# TAX FACTS

# TAX FACTS

## 1996/97 EDITION

A QUICK AND EASY GUIDE TO YOUR BUSINESS AND PERSONAL TAX MATTERS

KOGAN PAGE

KIDSONS IMPEY Chartered Accountants

First published in 1992

Reprinted in 1992

Second edition 1993
Third edition 1994
Fourth edition 1995
Fifth edition 1996

Apart from any fair dealing for the purposes of research or private study, or criticism or review, as permitted under the Copyright, Designs and Patents Act, 1988, this publication may only be reproduced, stored or transmitted, in any form or by any means, with the prior permission in writing of the publishers, or in the case of reprographic reproduction in accordance with the terms of licences issued by the Copyright Licensing Agency. Enquiries concerning reproduction outside those terms should be sent to the publishers at the undermentioned address:

Kogan Page Limited
120 Pentonville Road
London N1 9JN

© Kidsons Impey, Chartered Accountants, 1992, 1993, 1994, 1995, 1996

**British Library Cataloguing in Publication Data**
A CIP record for this book is available from the British Library.

ISBN 0 7494 2024 3

Typeset by Saxon Graphics Ltd, Derby
Printed in England by Clays Ltd, St Ives plc

# Contents

**List of Tables**     11

**Preface**     13

**Introduction**     15

**1 The Budget**     17

   *Introduction to Self Assessment 19*
      Outline 19; Date of Introduction 19; The Return 19; Late Return and Penalties 19; Payment of Taxes 20; Correction of Self Assessments 21; Inland Revenue Enquiry 21; Interest and Surcharges 21; Basis of Assessment of Income 22

**2 Income Tax**     23

   *Overview 23*

   *Tax Returns and PAYE 24*

   *Personal Allowances and Reliefs 25*
      Personal Allowance 25; Married Couple's Allowance 25; Age Allowance 26

   *Rates 26*

   *Exemptions 27*
      Social Security Benefits 29; Personal Equity Plans (PEPs) 29; Tax-exempt Special Savings Accounts (TESSAs) 30

   *The Family 31*
      Married Couples 31; Children 32

   *Settlements 32*
      Interest in Possession Trust 33; Accumulation and Maintenance Trusts 33; Discretionary Trusts 33

   *Charities 33*

   *Deductions 34*

Maintenance Payments in Separation or Divorce 34; Payroll Giving Schemes 34; Charitable Covenants 34; Gift Aid 35; Life Assurance Policies 35; Private Medical Insurance 37; Occupational Pension Schemes 37; Personal Pension Schemes 38; Relief for Interest Paid 40; Mortgage Interest Relief at Source (MIRAS) 41; Rent a Room Relief 41; Vocational Training 41; The Enterprise Investment Scheme 41; Venture Capital Trusts 44; The Business Expansion Scheme (BES) 45

*Tax Payment Dates and Interest* 46
Interest On Repayments ('Repayment Supplement') 46; From 1996/97 47; Due Dates For Payment 47; Interest on Overdue Tax 47; Rates of Interest 49; Certificates of Tax Deposit 49

*Types of Income* 49
Domicile, Residence and Ordinary Residence 51; Income from Abroad (Schedule D, Cases IV and V) 53; Schedule A 53; Premiums on Leases 55; Furnished Holiday Lettings 55; Schedule E 55; Profit-related Pay 56; Benefits in Kind 57; Other Emoluments 58; Company Cars 60

*Share Schemes* 61
Savings-related Share Option Schemes (SAYEs) 61; Non-savings-related Share Option Schemes 61; Approved Profit-sharing Schemes 61; Employee Share Ownership Plans (ESOPs) 62

*Anti-Avoidance Laws* 63

## 3  Business Tax                                                64

*Overview* 64

*Profits* 64

*Adjustments to Profit* 65

*Capital Expenditure* 66

*Income tax of Trades, Professions and Vocations*
  *for Partnerships and Sole Traders* 66
Trades, Professions and Vocations for Partnerships and Sole Traders (Schedule D, Cases I and II) 66; Business Losses 68; Partnership assessments 70

*Sub-contractors in the Construction Industry* 70

*Farming and Agricultural Profit* 71
Farming Profits 71; Herd Basis 72

*Commercial Woodlands* 73

*Capital Allowances* 73
Private Cars 76
Business Economic Notes 76

Contents/7

## 4 National Insurance — 77

*Overview* 77
*Class 1* 78
*Class 3* 78
*Classes 2 and 4 – the Self-employed* 79
*Maximum Contributions* 79
*Company Cars – Class 1A* 79

## 5 Corporation Tax — 81

*Overview* 81
*Rates* 82
    Advance Corporation Tax (ACT) 82; Pay and File 83
*Close Companies* 84
    Loans to Participators 84
*Purchase of Own Shares by an Unquoted Trading Company* 85

## 6 Capital Gains Tax — 86

*Overview* 86
*Self Assessment* 87
*Indexation* 87
*Rates* 88
*Payment* 88
*Chargeable Assets and Exemptions* 88
    Annual Exemption 89; Losses 90; Death 90; Husband and Wife 90; Principal Private Residence 91; Replacement of Business Assets (Rollover Relief 1) 92; Incorporation of Business (Rollover Relief 2) 93; Re-investment Relief (Rollover Relief 3) 93; Part Disposals of Land 94; Compulsory Purchase of Land 94; Holdover Relief 94; Registered Housing Associations 95; Non-residence 95; Retirement 95

## 7 Inheritance Tax — 97

*Overview* 97
*Transfer of Value* 98
*Returns* 99
*Rates* 99
    Nil Rate Band 99; Tax on Death 99; Quick Succession Relief 100

*8/Tax Facts*

*Payment 100*
Tax Payable by Instalments 101; Rates of Interest on Overdue Tax 101

*Spouses 101*

*Lifetime Gifts 102*
Gifts more than seven years before death 102; Gifts within seven years of death 102

*Gifts with Reservation 103*

*Exemptions – Exempt transfers 104*
Seven-year Write-off 104; Spouse 104; Annual Exemptions 104; Small Gifts 105; Normal Expenditure 105; Other Exemptions and Reliefs 105

*Business Property Relief 105*
Business Transfers and their Value 107; Related property 107; Lloyd's Underwriters 107; Woodlands 108; Farming 108

*Wills and Intestacy 109*
Wills 109; Intestacy 110

*Insurance 112*
Term Assurance 112; Funding Liability 113; Back to Back 113; Pensions 113

*Trusts 114*
Interest in Possession Trusts 114; Discretionary Trusts 114; Accumulation and Maintenance Trusts 115; Reversions 115; Resident and Non-Resident Trusts 115

*Overseas Aspects 115*
Domicile 115; Deemed Domicile 116; Non-UK Assets 116; UK Gilts 116; Trusts 116; Non-domiciled Spouse 116

## 8 Value Added Tax (VAT) 117

*Overview 117*

*Registration 118*
Taxable and Exempt Supplies 119; Planning points 119; Groups of companies 120; Application for Registration 120; Separation of Business Activities 120

*Taxable Supplies 121*
Value of Supplies 122

*Purchases 122*
Subsistence Expenses 123; Mileage Allowances 124

*Imports and Exports 124*
Imports 124; Exports 124

*Land and Buildings* 125
   The Option to Tax 126; Planning points 126
*Partially Exempt Traders* 126
   Capital Goods Scheme 127
*Bad Debt Relief* 127
*Accounting Records* 128
   Sales 128; Purchases 129; VAT Account 129; Retention of records 129; Retail Schemes 129; Cash Accounting 130; Annual Accounting 131
*Private Petrol Benefit* 132
*Administration* 133
   Returns 133; Planning Points 135; Notifying Changes 135; Penalties 136; Visits and Disputes 138

**9 Stamp Duty**   141

**10 Tax Planning**   143

*Overview* 143

*Income Tax* 143
   Home Purchases 143; Employee Share Schemes 144; Tax Repayments 144; Husband and Wife 144; Children's Investments 145; Other Interest Relief 145; Retirement 145; Company Cars 146; Mobile Phones 147; Interest-free Loans 147; In-house Services for Employees 147; Award Schemes for Employees 147; Speeding Tax Relief 148; Unquoted Trading Companies 148; Offshore Currency Funds 148; Working Abroad 148; Pension Schemes 149; Additional Voluntary Contributions (AVCs) 150; Business Profits 150; Additional Routes 150

*Corporation Tax* 151
   Deferral of Income 151; Acceleration of expenditure 151; Other planning points 152

*Capital Gains Tax* 153
   Rates of Capital Gains Tax 153; Trusts and Capital Gains Tax 153; Planning Sales 153; Second Homes 154; Rollover and Retirement Reliefs 154; Share Exchanges 155; Profits 156; Business Assets Held Outside the Company 156

*Inheritance Tax* 156
   Lifetime Gifts 157; Accumulation and Maintenance Settlements 157; Seven-year Rule 157; Reservation of Benefit 157; Exemptions 157; Business and Agricultural Property Relief 158; Shares in Private

## 10/Tax Facts

Companies 158; Wills and the Nil Rate Band 158; Insurance 159; Assets that will Increase in Value 159; Retaining Flexibility 159; Trusts 159

**Appendix I   Taxpayer's Charter**                                               161

**Appendix II   Official Errors**                                                 163

**Kidsons Impey Offices and Contacts**                                            165

# List of Tables

| | | |
|---|---|---|
| 1 | Income tax allowances | 26 |
| 2 | Rates and bands of Income Tax | 27 |
| 3 | Taxable and exempt Social Securities benefits | 29 |
| 4 | Contributions to personal pension plans 1989/90 – 1996/97 by age | 40 |
| 5 | The maximum incomes on which pension contributions can be assessed | 40 |
| 6 | Borrowings where the interest paid qualifies for income tax relief | 42 |
| 7 | Income schedules and due dates | 48 |
| 8 | Rates of interest for the repayment supplement and an overdue tax | 49 |
| 9 | The bases on which various types of income are assessed | 50 |
| 10 | The assessment of income from abroad | 54 |
| 11 | The prescribed rates of interest for assessing benefits in kind and beneficial loans | 59 |
| 12 | Fuel scale charges – Income tax (1996/97) | 60 |
| 13 | Employee car and van benefits | 60 |
| 14 | Industrial building allowances | 75 |
| 15 | Plant and machinery allowances | 75 |
| 16 | The weekly rates of NI Class 1 contributions (1996/97) | 78 |
| 17 | Fuel scale charges – National Insurance (1996/97) | 80 |
| 18 | Corporation tax rates for the four years ending 31 March 1997 | 83 |
| 19 | The retail price index 1984–95 | 87 |

# 12/Tax Facts

| 20 | Inheritance tax due dates | 100 |
| 21 | The tapering relief for gifts made 3–7 years before death | 103 |
| 22 | Business property relief | 106 |
| 23 | Intestacy rules | 111 |
| 24 | Intestacy rules in Scotland | 112 |
| 25 | The VAT charges for the private use of company cars | 133 |
| 26 | The stamp duty on conveyances and sales | 141 |
| 27 | Percentages of tax arrears waived because of official errors | 163 |

# Preface

This book has been written to provide an easily readable guide to taxation in the UK for both individuals and companies. Many books on taxation are difficult to follow or highly detailed in technical matters, and this can be off-putting to non-specialists wishing to understand their taxation position. What most readers want to know is how tax planning will work for *them*; and how best to minimise the tax they pay.

We hope that readers will find this book of practical use, now and in the future.

Graham Kidson, Tax Partner
Kidsons Impey, December 1995

# Introduction

*Tax Facts* is intended to provide a straightforward and comprehensible guide to the principal taxes of the UK. By looking at all aspects of personal and commercial taxation, the book will serve as a fully-rounded guide for everyone interested in the money-saving aspects of tax planning. Written in a clear, jargon-free style, it will provide all those with a non-financial background with an immediate explanation of the various taxes and their ramifications.

Chapter One provides a description of the 1995 November Budget, the main provisions of which apply from 6 April 1996. This chapter also includes a summary of the major changes arising on the introduction of Self Assessment as well as the new rules for taxing income rather than the more complex arrangements presently in force. The remaining chapters are each devoted to the principal areas of taxation: national insurance; corporation tax; value added tax; inheritance tax and so on. At the end of the book the reader will find a useful chapter on tax saving tips. Given that income tax is the main tax, Chapter Two, which is devoted to it, is more extensive and covers aspects that impinge on the other taxes. Chapter Three covers the area of business tax and the tax paid on business profits.

*Tax Facts* is absolutely up-to-date with the changes announced in the Budget of November 1995, although the provisions of that Budget have not yet been legally ratified and there may be other changes introduced as the proposals pass through Parliament.

While the intention here is to be as comprehensive as possible, taxation is a complex and difficult area. *Tax Facts* will serve as a good basic introduction but the reader is also recommended to seek professional independent advice before implementing any steps aimed at tax planning.

# 1

# The Budget

This is essentially a political Budget calculated to stave off any criticism of the tax reductions, which benefit all levels of taxpayers, by channelling additional resources into 'middle England's' most popular causes—health, education and law and order.

It is notable for its relative dearth of technical changes in all forms of taxation, with the emphasis on rates of tax such as the reductions in basic rate income tax from 25 per cent to 24 per cent, and the corresponding reduction of the small companies charge to corporation tax from 25 per cent to 24 per cent.

One or two niche planning areas are identifiable. The first is the trend towards more flexible retirement planning, as evidenced in the Chancellor's measures to extend capital gains tax retirement relief for company owners selling up by reducing the qualifying age from 55 to 50. Now that company owners can simultaneously sell their company and uplift their pension benefits, the planning options for business owners are considerably increased, particularly when account is taken of the various tax reliefs available on the reinvestment of funds arising from the sale of the business in suitable new business opportunities.

For minority shareholders in private companies (those holding less than 26 per cent), the introduction of 100 per cent inheritance tax relief also clarifies the planning position. Doubts about giving away prior to or on death are resolved in favour of the latter, subject to the major caveat, as with all current planning issues, that a change in government may herald a substantially different tax regime.

There was some evidence of the wish to take more people out of the tax net, so in the main the increase in tax allowances was greater than inflation. The greatest increase was in the nil rate band for inheritance tax which increases from £154,000 to £200,000 with effect from 6 April 1996. This will greatly reduce the number of persons who fall into the category of paying inheritance tax on their estate on death simply as a result of the value of their property.

There are several areas of interest to all those who save to meet the costs of old age, one of which is the introduction of a 20 per cent band for all saving income for all taxpayers who pay tax below the higher rate of 40 per cent. One area of concern for all is the effect of the high cost of healthcare or residential homes for the elderly. Here the prudent person who has saved for their old age is forced to meet the costs of residential care from their private means, while another person who spent all their savings has residential care paid for by the state. At present a person with assets including savings of less than £3,000 is not asked to make any contribution while people with more than £8,000 must meet the entire cost themselves. From 6 April it is intended that these limits be increased to £8,000 and £16,000 respectively. There is also an intention to review pensions legislation so that the pension can be drawn in line with likely need where greater funds may be needed in old age, rather than on the current basis where the pension at best merely keeps pace with inflation.

The Chancellor has indicated that he would wish to reduce the basic rate of income tax to 20 per cent and abolish capital gains tax completely. It is difficult to see either of these goals being reached in the short term either because of the problems of sensible funding or because of the inherent difficulties of complete abolition of capital taxes. Should it occur, the abolition of capital taxes is likely to lead to additional complexities in tax legislation with the area of difficulty being the boundaries between the definition of an income or a capital profit. The income profit would be taxable while the capital gain would not.

As for simplification in the tax system, Utopia still seems as far away as ever! The one measure of simplification announced was the intention for the Inland Revenue to write most of the basic tax law in plain user friendly language. There did not appear to be a similar announcement by Customs and Excise. Simplification here would be welcome since so much of VAT is determined by Statutory Instrument rather than primary legislation.

There were the annual increases in tobacco and fuel duties. While the Chancellor did not increase the basic duties on wine and beer, there was one surprise in that he decreased the duty on spirits. This is the first such decrease in such duties for many a year.

It was a fairly prudent Budget if you accept the Chancellor's assumption that the United Kingdom is moving towards a balanced budget, where government income equates to government spending. This is now targeted for the end of the decade. It does however seem that this Budget is intended to be a prudent look towards the possibility that interest rates fall slightly over the coming months, enabling the Chancellor to be more generous next year while still appearing to be acting cautiously and prudently.

The present tax rules on capital gains tax and inheritance tax as they affect the owners of private companies are more generous than at any time in the last 50 years. It is difficult to see the Chancellor's economic predictions coming to fulfilment and at the same time meeting with public acceptance, so it is doubtful that such generous rules can continue indefinitely. The private shareholder must therefore carefully consider his options and his longer-term intentions regarding such shareholdings and plan how to maximise his investment's potential.

## Introduction to Self Assessment

### *Outline*

There are to be fundamental changes to the tax system in the future. They come under two prime headings. These are the introduction of Self Assessment and the simplification of the methods used to decide what business and investment income is to be taxed in any particular year.

Self Assessment will cover new rules for the payment of tax, making of returns and the arrangements the Inland Revenue has for running the tax system. The aim is to simplify the system so that the taxpayer will be able to complete his tax return, compute his own tax liabilities, and pay his tax, thereby reducing the burden on the Inland Revenue.

### *Date of Introduction*

Self Assessment is to be introduced in the tax year 1996/97 which starts on 6 April 1996. It will affect all individuals, as well as executors, trustees, personal representatives, letting agents and partners in a partnership who pay income tax and capital gains tax.

### *The Return*

The heart of the new regime will be the tax return. The new return will include a section which will work out the amount of tax to pay and this will be the assessment of the taxpayer's liability. It is not, however, necessary for the assessment section to be completed and it will be possible to submit the return uncompleted, leaving the assessment to be made by the Inland Revenue.

The new returns for 1996/97 will be issued in April 1997. Where the taxpayer completes the Self Assessment, his return should be returned duly completed to the Inland Revenue by 31 January 1998 or within three months where the Inland Revenue issues the return after 31 October 1997. If the taxpayer does not complete the Self Assessment section of the return it should be completed by 30 September 1997 or within two months if the return is issued after 31 July 1997.

### *Late Returns and Penalties*

When a return is submitted late there will be an automatic penalty of

£100 unless there is a reasonable excuse. If the return is six months late another automatic penalty of £100 will be due. There are even more stringent penalties that the Inland Revenue can invoke to encourage the taxpayer to complete the return. Furthermore, the Inspector of Taxes can, within five years, determine tax due based on his information and understanding. This will be payable by the taxpayer without appeal. However, it will be automatically superseded when the return is submitted.

## *Payment of Taxes*

Tax on all the different sources of income which are currently paid on a variety of dates will now all come together in a single payment regime. Each taxpayer will have their own tax account with the Inland Revenue to which all taxes, including penalties and interest, will be added. The taxes collected will cover income tax and capital gains tax. The main date most taxpayers will pay tax will be on 31 January following the end of the tax year. Where a return is issued after 31 October the payment date will be three months after issue.

In certain circumstances, interim tax payments on account will be due on 31 January in the tax year and on 31 July following the end of the tax year. For the tax year 1996/97 this would mean 31 January and 31 July 1997. This means that the final payment for 1996/97 due on 31 January 1998 would be the amount of the self-assessment less payments on account and any tax deductions.

Tax deductions at source will continue to be the principal method of tax payment. This means that the income received from employment will continue to be paid via the PAYE system. In addition, dividend income and interest paid will continue to be paid net, after tax has been deducted at source by the financial institutions. These arrangements remain in force and are in no way affected by the introduction of self-assessment.

The two interim payments on account are based on the income of the previous year. Each payment is based on half the total tax liabilities less any tax deducted at source. The taxpayer can reduce the amount of the interim payments where he understands that the amount due in the year will be less. This can arise where the income in the year is lower than in the previous year. No interim payments will be due if the tax due falls below a de minimis level or below a specified proportion of total income. The intention is to set these levels by statutory instrument to ensure that the interim payment system is used only in cases where larger amounts of tax are due. There are no interim payments of capital gains tax required as the entire liability to capital gains tax is due on 31 January following the tax year.

## Correction of Self Assessments

The inspector may amend a Self Assessment to correct obvious errors at any time within nine months of submission of the return. This process is referred to as 'repairs'. The intention is to allow amendments where there is no dispute over the correction. The taxpayer may amend his return at any time within a year of submission. These procedures are quite separate from the amendments made to a Self Assessment as a result of Inland Revenue enquiries.

The basis of Self Assessment is that the Inland Revenue will rely upon the taxpayer and will restrict their enquiries. The Inland Revenue may, however, wish to make enquiries into certain returns. This will be done on three grounds, which are that they hold information that warrants further inquiry, the returns contain certain unsatisfactory features that warrant further enquiry or on the basis of a random selection. To start an enquiry the Inspector must issue a notice within a year of the date of submission of the return or amendment. However, where a return or amendment is late, the Inspector has a little longer to instigate enquiries as he must do so by the quarter date following the anniversary of a late return or amendment. In the course of the enquiries the Inspector can call for documents and accounts and other information to help him decide if the return or amendment is correct and complete.

## Inland Revenue Enquiry

When the enquiry is complete the Inland Revenue will issue a formal notice. The notice will include the Inspector's calculation of tax that should be assessed. The taxpayer may appeal against such a notice and has a period of 30 days in which to do so. In the following 30 days the Inland Revenue may issue an amendment to the Self Assessment. If the taxpayer does not agree with the Inland Revenue's conclusion he may appeal to the Commissioner in a manner similar to those presently in existence.

## Interest and Surcharges

Where tax is paid late there is a system of interest. Interest is payable on any tax paid after the due date. Interest is payable where interim payments are made late. Interest is also charged when surcharges and penalties are paid late. In addition to interest, the new regime also incorporates surcharges to encourage the taxpayer to pay. A surcharge is payable, as well as interest, when a payment is made after the due date. A surcharge of 5 per cent of the tax outstanding is made if the tax is paid more than 28 days late. A further charge of 5 per cent is also made where payment is made more than 6 months after the due date. The Inland Revenue will pay interest on overpayments from the due date or the date of actual payment if this is later.

In the 1994 Budget the Chancellor announced that he intended to introduce systems allowing for the electronic submission of returns. It is hoped that this will apply to company tax returns by the end of 1996 and be extended to individuals at the start of Self Assessment in April 1997 when the first Self Assessment returns are issued by the Inland Revenue.

## Basis of Assessment of Income

The basis on which trading income is currently assessed is very complex. (See page 66). The income on interest and annuities and annual payments, where tax is not deducted at source, is taxed on the basis of income of the prior year. This is called the prior year basis. (See page 67). Self Assessment would not be viable if these complex rules were retained. Under Self Assessment the basis of assessment will be the income of the year. This is called the current year basis.

In practice the current year basis for business profits (sole traders and partnerships) will start for the tax year 1997/98. Where the business starts up after 6 April 1994 the current year basis is used from the start. Where the existing business is trading before 6 April 1994 there are transitional arrangements. Such arrangements allow the business to average its profits over the years up to 1997/98. This enables the transition from the current basis of assessment, based on profits arising in the accounting year that end in the preceding tax year, to be fairly implemented. In practice, in the transitional period up to 1997/98, two year's trading will be averaged and treated as one tax year. The transitional arrangements are highly complex and the Budget includes outline avoidance measures to prevent taxpayers taking advantage of the averaging process to artificially avoid paying tax.

# 2

# Income Tax

Overview — Tax returns and PAYE — Personal allowances and reliefs — Rates — Exemptions — The family — Settlements — Charities — Deductions — Tax payment dates and interest — Types of income — Share Schemes — Anti Avoidance Laws

### Overview

Income tax, introduced in 1799, is the principal tax in the United Kingdom and raises greater revenue for the government than even VAT or national insurance. Originally 10p in the £, the rates have climbed steadily over the years to reach levels as high as 98p in the £ in the 1960s, falling in the 1980s. The basic rate of income tax is now reduced to 24p in the £, with a higher rate of 40p, and a lower rate of 20p in the £.

Income tax is progressive in that on the lower incomes, once allowances are exceeded, tax is paid at 20p in the £; if taxable income is over £3,900 it is paid at 24p in the £ and over £25,500 it is paid at 40p in the £. Every man, woman and child is subject to tax on their income per year, with the income tax year running from 6 April to 5 April in the following year.

To ascertain the amount of tax that every individual must pay you have to establish his *total income*. This is not as simple as it sounds since income comes from a variety of sources and for each different source there can be a different way of determining the amount that is taxable. A few types of income are exempt from tax. The assessable income from the various sources is totalled and certain *deductions* may then be made.

Having reduced the total income by the allowable deductions, the first slice of the net income will suffer no tax. The size of this slice depends on the personal circumstances of the taxpayer and his tax *allowances and reliefs*. Income tax is then charged for the tax year in question in accordance with the set *rates*.

## 24/Tax Facts

Tax relief on the married couple's allowance is restricted to 15 per cent, as is the tax relief on mortgage interest relief on loans of up to £30,000. This indicates the intention to limit the benefit of allowances so that all receive the same benefit, be they higher rate taxpayers or not.

The Chancellor introduced in his November 1993 Budget measures to simplify income tax. These changes will come into effect in 1996/97. The new system will enable the tax payer to work out his or her own tax bill, receiving one tax statement and one tax bill. Until then the existing complex arrangements continue. The arrangements covering the transitional period until 1996/97 are complex. They are set out more fully in Chapter 1 under 'Self Assessment'.

### Tax Returns and PAYE

Under the existing system, at the start of each tax year the Inland Revenue sends out tax returns. Recipients are asked to fill in the form, giving details of income for the previous year, and of the tax allowances they will be claiming for the coming year. The form should then be signed, dated, and returned to the Inland Revenue.

The new Self Assessment system is introduced with effect from 1996/97. Under this new system individuals are required to file their return by 31 January following the end of the tax year. The return is designed so that the taxpayer can calculate his own tax liability. However, he can request the Inland Revenue to do this for him if he files his return earlier, by 1 October following the end of the tax year.

For the first year (1996/97) the following filing dates will apply:

| Return Issued | Filing Date |
| --- | --- |
| Issued before 1.11.97 | 31.1.98 |
| Issued after 31.10.97 | 3 months after issue |
| IR to calculate tax and issued before 1.8.97 | 30.9.97 |
| IR to calculate tax and issued after 31.7.97 | 2 months after issue |

If no tax return is issued then a taxpayer must notify chargeability to income or capital gains tax within six months of the end of the tax year.

Tax will be payable in three instalments:

- 31 January in tax year.
- 31 July after the tax year.
- 31 January following the tax year.

The first two instalments are calculated as 50 per cent of the previous year's liability; the third payment is the final balancing figure.

For 1996/97, payments will be as follows:

- 31 January 1997: 50 per cent of income tax paid in 1995/96 excluding higher rate tax on taxed income, PAYE and tax deducted at source.
- 31 July 1997: 50 per cent as above
- 31 January 1998: Balance of 1996/97 tax, including CGT, sent with the return.

Note: the higher rate tax on taxed income and capital gains tax for 1995/96 will be payable on 1 December 1996 under the 'old' system.

A common method of tax payment is the PAYE system. Most people who are not self-employed will be paid by their employer under the PAYE system. Tax is deducted from employees' wages by the employer, and paid monthly to the Inland Revenue. This continues under the Self Assessment system.

## Personal Allowances and Reliefs

Everyone is allowed a certain level of income before tax is due. These allowances or reliefs vary according to individual circumstances, and are set out in Table 1.

### *Personal allowance*

Every individual taxpayer, married or single, is entitled to a personal allowance. This can be set in full against any income, either earned or unearned.

### *Married couple's allowance*

This is in addition to the personal allowance and will automatically be given to the husband in the first instance. If he is unable to make full use of the allowance, the unused balance may be transferred to the wife and set against the wife's income. There are special rules for calculating the unused balance. The husband must make an irrevocable election for the transfer within six years of the end of the tax year. The wife has an automatic right to claim half this allowance irrespective of the husband's wishes or the tax efficiency of such a claim. Alternatively on a joint election the whole allowance can be transferred to the wife. From 6 April 1995 tax relief on the married couple's allowance is restricted to 15 per cent.

## 26/Tax Facts

Table 1  *Income tax allowances*

|  | 1994/95 £ | 1995/96 £ | 1996/7 £ |
|---|---|---|---|
| **Personal allowance** |  |  |  |
| Under 65 | 3,445 | 3,525 | 3,765 |
| 65–74 | 4,200 | 4,630 | 4,910 |
| 75 and over | 4,370 | 4,800 | 5,090 |
| **Married couple's allowance** |  |  |  |
| Under 65* | 1,720 | 1,720 | 1,790 |
| 65–74* | 2,665 | 2,995 | 3,115 |
| 75 and over* | 2,705 | 3,035 | 3,155 |
| **Maximum income before abatement of reliefs for over 65s** | 14,200 | 14,600 | 15,200 |
| **Additional personal allowances** |  |  |  |
| Single-handed responsibility for a child* | 1,720 | 1,720 | 1,790 |
| Blind person | 1,200 | 1,200 | 1,250 |
| Widow's bereavement* | 1,720 | 1,720 | 1,790 |

\* Allowances where relief is restricted to 15 per cent in 1996/97

## Age allowance

Taxpayers who are aged 65 or over in a tax year are entitled to higher personal and married couple's allowances as set out in Table 1. For a married couple, the level of married couple's allowance will depend on the age of the older spouse. If the husband is aged 71, but the wife is 76 (for example), the married couple's allowance is £3,155 for 1996/97 (based on the wife's age).

The extra relief for the older taxpayer will be proportionately reduced once a person's level of income exceeds £15,200. For every £2 of income received in excess of this amount, the higher allowance is reduced by £1, until it reaches the level of relief given to a person *under* the age of 65, which is the minimum entitlement. The over 65s' married couple's allowance will be reduced in the same way if the individual's taxable income exceeds £15,200.

## Rates

Income is divided into bands with the lower bands bearing tax at lower rates and the higher bands at higher rates. These bands are set out in Table 2.

Table 2 *Rates and bands of Income Tax*

| Band of taxable income £ | Rate of tax % | Total taxable income to top of band £ | Total tax to top of band £ |
|---|---|---|---|
| **1996/97** | | | |
| First 3,900 | 20 | 3,900 | 780 |
| Next 21,600 | 24 | 25,500 | 5,964 |
| Remainder | 40 | | |
| **1995/96** | | | |
| First 3,200 | 20 | 3,200 | 640 |
| Next 21,100 | 25 | 24,300 | 5,915 |
| Remainder | 40 | | |
| **1994/95** | | | |
| First 3,000 | 20 | 3,000 | 600 |
| Next 20,700 | 25 | 23,700 | 5,775 |
| Remainder | 40 | | |

Under new proposals that come into effect from 6 April 1996, a rate of tax of 20 per cent will apply on most income from savings, in so far as that income would not be subject to the higher rate of income tax which starts on taxable income in excess of £25,500. The effect of this measure is to ensure that taxpayers who are only subject to basic rate tax of 24 per cent on their earned income will be liable to only 20 per cent on income from savings. Income from savings includes interest from banks and building societies, as well as distributions from unit trusts. Dividend income from companies is already only taxed at the rate of 20 per cent.

## Exemptions

Some forms of income are exempt from tax (either by statute or by extra-statutory concession). These are listed below. Further explanation will be found later in the book.

- Interest on National Savings Certificates (up to the maximum permitted holding).
- Interest and bonus on 'save as you earn' schemes.
- Supplement received on tax repayments (including inheritance tax).
- Interest on damages for personal injuries.
- The first £70 of interest from a National Savings Bank Ordinary Deposit Account.
- Scholarship income. (But in some cases where the income is provided by the employer of the scholar's parent, the parent may be assessable under the 'benefit-in-kind' provisions).
- Private sickness benefit schemes and health, accident, disability, infirmity and unemployment insurance policies which provide replacement income to compensate the policy holder whose earnings fall as a result of ill-health, disability, accident or unemployment. This exemption does not apply to a scheme provided by a person's employer.

- Certain lump sums under pension arrangements or retirement annuity contracts.
- Compensation for loss of office up to £30,000 and certain other terminal payments.
- Wages in lieu of notice.
- Redundancy payments up to statutory limits.
- Luncheon vouchers up to 15p per day and subject to certain conditions.
- Long service awards, other than cash, for service of over 20 years up to a value of £20 for each year of service.
- Foreign service allowance to Crown servants.
- Travel expenses paid to a person employed abroad for a continuous period of 60 days or more to enable him to visit a spouse or child (or travel expenses of spouse or child to visit such person).
- Board and lodging expenses paid to an employee whose duties are performed wholly abroad.
- Annuities and pension additions to holders of the VC and certain other Gallantry awards.
- Certain annuities paid by Germany or Austria to victims of Nazi persecution.
- Certain allowances, bounties, etc, paid to military reservists.
- Some income of foreign residents exempted under double taxation agreements.
- Interest on certain UK Government stocks held by non-residents.
- Adoption allowances approved under the Children's Act 1975.
- Certain Social Security benefits (see Table 3).
- There are several schemes to encourage employee shareholdings in companies. This can be by way of: savings schemes; share options; or direct provision by the employer of funds which trustees can use to acquire shares on behalf of employees. Provided Inland Revenue approval is obtained and various conditions are followed, the profits under such schemes will not be taxed as income.
- Dividends and interest from personal equity plans (PEPs).
- Profit-related pay (PRP) under a scheme approved by the Inland Revenue.
- Certain maintenance payments from a former spouse.
- Interest and bonus payments on tax-exempt special savings accounts (TESSAs).
- Betting winnings including Premium Bond prizes.
- Profits from commercial forestry.
- Outplacement counselling (help for redundant employees).
- Income from Venture Capital Trusts.
- Relocation expenses paid by employers up to £8,000.
- Payment by employers of employee liability insurance.
- Payment by employers of up to £5 per night per employee towards miscellaneous overnight expenditure.
- Payments made for mis-sold personal pensions during the period covered by the Securities and Investment Board.

## Social Security Benefits

Certain Social Security benefits are taxable and others are not, as listed in Table 3.

Table 3 *Taxable and exempt Social Security benefits*

| Exempt from tax | Taxable |
|---|---|
| Attendance allowance | Income support (up to a set amount) to strikers and the unemployed |
| Child benefit |  |
| So much of any benefit as is attributable to an increase in respect of a child | Industrial death benefit |
| | Industrial disablement pension |
| Child's special allowance | Invalid care allowance |
| Council tax benefit | Invalid care allowance when paid with retirement pension |
| Dependency | |
| Disability living allowance including Care and Mobility component | Retirement pension |
| | Statutory maternity pay |
| | Statutory sick pay |
| Disability working allowance | Unemployment benefit |
| Family credit | Widow's pension |
| Guardian's allowance | Widowed mother's allowance |
| Hospital downrating | |
| Housing benefit | |
| Incapacity benefit (middle and highest rate taxable for new claimants from 6 April 1995) | |
| Income support except where taxable (see next column) | |
| Maternity allowance | |
| One parent benefit | |
| Pneumoconiosis, byssinosis workmen's compensation and other schemes | |
| Severe disablement allowance | |
| Social fund | |
| Widow's payment | |

## Personal Equity Plans (PEPs)

Personal equity plans were introduced on 1 January 1987 and are intended to encourage individuals to invest in (mainly) UK and EC businesses by offering tax advantages to investors. The Chancellor extended from 5 April 1995 the range of investments covered by this relief from equity investments to include corporate bonds, convertibles and preference shares and certain European stocks.

The advantages are that income earned from investments within a plan is exempt from income tax, and capital gains made on disposal of shares within the plan are exempt from capital gains tax. Investors in approved plans do not need to declare such income or gains on their tax returns. Plans are run by Treasury-approved managers and there are a wide range of these including stockbrokers, unit trust groups, insurance companies, banks and building societies. Their charges are based on the value of the plan.

Some plans allow individual investors freedom to select the companies in which investment is made. With others, all investment decisions are left to the plan managers.

Investors must be 18 or over and (except for Crown servants) must be resident and ordinarily resident in the UK.

The scheme originally operated for calendar years, but from 6 April 1989 it operates for the fiscal year. The annual investment limit is £6,000. Husband and wife can each contribute and thus the maximum for a couple is £12,000.

Since January 1992 an additional amount up to £3,000 annually may be invested in a single company PEP in a UK or EC company. Plans may be used to invest in new share issues, including privatisation issues. As privatisation issues are made in personal names, an individual applies in his own name and transfers the allocation (to the extent that it does not take his total investment in a plan to over the permitted maximum) to the plan managers within 30 days of allocation.

Plan managers do not have to invest in equities immediately funds are received from investors. Cash may be placed on interest-bearing deposit for a period pending investment.

Potential investors must realise that there are manager's charges and that withdrawing money from a plan too soon may therefore be unwise.

## *Tax-exempt Special Savings Accounts (TESSAs)*

From 1 January 1991 each individual aged 18 years and above is entitled to open one 'Tax Exempt Special Savings Account' (TESSA) with a bank or building society. Investments in each account are limited to £3,000 in the first year and £1,800 in each subsequent year up to a maximum of £9,000 over five years. From 1 January 1996 an investor whose first TESSA has matured at the end of the five year period will be able to reinvest up to £9,000 in a second TESSA.

Interest on capital in the account will not be taxable provided the capital remains in the account for five years. Interest will be credited to the account gross, but only the net of tax equivalent can be withdrawn during the five-year term. Regular or irregular sums may be deposited in a TESSA, but if capital is withdrawn during the five-year period, tax advantages are lost.

## The Family

### *Married Couples*

Each spouse is separately responsible for paying tax and for claiming allowances, reliefs and deductions and receiving refunds. Each spouse is also responsible for making a 'return of income'.

Every individual is entitled to a personal allowance. This can be set against all income, either from earnings or from investments. A married woman's state pension ranks as her income even if she receives it by virtue of her husband's contributions. If either spouse is entitled to an occupational pension and, under the rules of the relevant scheme, allocates some part of it to the spouse that part will be treated as the income of the spouse.

The amount of allowance is graded according to age at the end of the tax year (see Table 1). Thus a person whose 65th birthday is 5 April 1997 will be entitled to the 65-75 allowance for tax year 1996/97. The allowance will be due even if the individual should die before his 65th birthday.

Every married man living with or voluntarily maintaining his wife is also entitled to a married couple's allowance. Again, there are three levels and to decide which is appropriate, the age of the elder spouse is taken into account. If the husband has insufficient income to take full advantage of his personal allowance and the married couple's allowance, he can transfer the unused part of the married couple's allowance to his wife. The wife can claim half this allowance or the couple can choose to allocate this allowance to either one of them or split it equally between them.

For the year of marriage the married couple's allowance is limited to one-twelfth of a full year's allowance for each month from the date of marriage until the following 5 April.

If there is separation or divorce, the husband will be entitled to the full year's married couple's allowance. In that year the wife is entitled to any of the married couple's allowance not used against her husband's income. Either partner may also be entitled to an additional personal allowance (which is equal to the under-65 married couple's allowance), if he or she has a child living with him or her after the separation or divorce. With effect from 6 April 1995 tax relief on these allowances was restricted to 15 per cent.

The widow's bereavement allowance may be available in addition to the additional personal allowance. Moreover, in the year of her husband's death, a widow will also be entitled to any balance of married couple's allowance not absorbed by her husband's income prior to his death. Relief for this too was restricted to 15 per cent from 6 April 1995.

If income arises in joint names it will be treated as belonging half each to the husband and wife. However, if it is possible to demonstrate that the capital giving rise to the income does not belong to each spouse equally and if both spouses sign a declaration to that effect, the income can be allocated differently. The declaration will only be effective as regards income arising from the date of declaration.

Some husbands may consider transferring substantial assets or funds to their wives (or vice versa) in order that each spouse has sufficient income to take maximum advantage of the allowances and sometimes in order to keep each individual's income within a lower band (see Table 2). This is acceptable, provided that the transfer is an outright unconditional gift. However, if the donor has the right to reclaim the asset or to dictate how it is dealt with, it is probable that the income arising will be regarded as that of the donor, not the donee.

As stated above, each spouse is entitled to their own allowances, reliefs and deductions. The exception is mortgage interest relief. In this case the spouses are able to sign a joint election to allocate the relief in whichever way they choose – regardless of which one actually pays the interest. If no election is signed, the relief is split equally between husband and wife.

Age allowance is reduced if income is above a certain figure. Each spouse is considered separately to see if any of the higher amounts of personal allowance should be withdrawn. When considering whether any of the higher amounts of married couple's allowance should be withdrawn, only the husband's income is considered. If his income is above the 'reduction figure' (see Table 1) his personal allowance is reduced first (but not below the under 65 rate of allowance) and then his married couple's allowance.

## *Children*

Children under the age of 18 receive the same allowances as adults and the same tax refunds if these are due.

It is now possible for parents to gift capital to their child and, provided the funds are given absolutely, the income derived therefrom will be taxed at the child's rate of income tax.

## Settlements

A settlement (or trust) is created when one person (the settlor) places funds or assets under the control of trustees for the benefit of a person or group of persons (the beneficiaries). The settlor may also be one of the trustees. For taxation purposes the trustees have an identity separate from the settlor and separate from their own personal affairs (see also Chapter 7).

Apart from pension funds (see page 37) probably the three most common forms of trust are:

- interest in possession trusts
- accumulation and maintenance trusts
- discretionary trusts.

Trusts are not entitled to the benefit of the 20 per cent rate of tax on the first £3,900 of taxable income.

## Interest in possession trust

An interest in possession trust broadly means that one or more individuals have a right to the income of the trust. Income tax is payable by the trustees at the rate of 24 per cent (if it has not already been taken at source, as is the case with shares, for example) and the trustees give the beneficiaries a voucher to certify that their share of the income has been taxed. Beneficiaries may then be chargeable at the higher rate or may be entitled to reclaim tax, depending on their total income from all sources and their allowances.

## Accumulation and maintenance trusts

Accumulation and maintenance trusts are used, as the name implies, to hold income, usually for minors, until a certain age is reached or funds are needed for their maintenance. The income of such a trust normally suffers tax at a rate of 34 per cent. When income is released, the voucher will indicate that it is a net amount after deductions of 34 per cent.

## Discretionary trusts

Discretionary trusts specify a group or category of beneficiaries but give the trustees discretion as to how income and/or capital is allocated within the group. Again the trustees must normally pay tax at the rate of 34 per cent.

Where a settlement is revocable or in other circumstances where the settlor may benefit from the settlement, the income will be treated as his and taxed at his personal tax rate.

# Charities

An approved charity can claim exemption from income tax on investment income which is used for charitable purposes. It can also claim exemption on trading income, if the trade is exercised in the course of carrying out a primary purpose of the charity or if the work in connection with the trade is mainly carried out by beneficiaries of the charity. Exemption from capital gains tax is also available if the gain is used for charitable purposes.

If a trader seconds an employee to work temporarily for a charity, he may still treat the costs of employing that person as a trading expense.

A group of individuals who raise funds to support a charity (by bazaars, jumble sales, etc) are not statutorily exempt from tax on their trading income, but by concession the Inland Revenue does not charge tax if the following conditions apply:

1. The organisation is not regularly trading.
2. The trading is not in competition with other traders.
3. The activities are supported mainly because the public knows that the profits are for charity.
4. The profits are given to charity or used for charitable purposes.

## Deductions

### Maintenance Payments in Separation or Divorce

The tax treatment of maintenance payments to a former spouse depends on whether they began by virtue of court orders, or agreements, dated before or after 15 March 1988.

Before 15 March 1988: The payer made payments in full and was given tax relief by his tax inspector. However, tax relief for the payer is now limited to the amount to which he was entitled for 1988/89. The tax relief on the first £1,790 was restricted to 15 per cent from 6 April 1995.

After 14 March 1988: Payments are made in full and the recipient is exempt from tax on them. The payer gets tax relief for the payments up to a maximum of the basic married couple's allowance of £1,790. From 6 April 1995 the tax relief is restricted to 15 per cent.

### Payroll Giving Schemes

Employees are able to join a 'payroll giving scheme'. This enables any employee who wishes to join to make donations of up to £1,200 a year from 1996/97 onwards. The employer will deduct the donation from pay before operating PAYE and will pass the money to an approved agent who will pass it on to the nominated charity or charities.

### Charitable Covenants

Individuals are encouraged to assist charities by means of 'deeds of covenant'. These are documents under which the individual promises to pay a stipulated amount for a period which can exceed three years. It is normal to make them for four years. The individual then pays the full amount less tax at the basic rate. Sometimes deeds are made which stipulate a gross amount, say £100 pa, and so the payer gives the charity £76 (while the basic rate is 24 per cent). In other cases the deed might stipulate a net amount (ie a variable sum which after deduction of tax at the current basic rate gives a constant net figure).

In order that the charity may reclaim the tax deducted, it is necessary that the payment be gratuitous and not be a means of paying for some reciprocal benefits. No payment of the covenanted sum should be made before the deed is signed.

With some heritage and conservation charities (the National Trust, or say, the 'friends' of a museum), individuals who sign deeds of covenant may enjoy certain benefits. It has always been difficult to be certain whether such benefits imperil the tax benefit of the scheme. The 1989 Finance Act makes it clear that where the benefit is the right to view property (or to observe wildlife), the preservation of which is the sole or main purpose of the charity, such benefit will not nullify the tax benefit.

In some circumstances, if a person wishes to make an isolated donation to a charity, the donation can be made more valuable by means of a 'deposited covenant'. Broadly, this means that the gift is treated as four separate payments due in four succeeding years, but is paid all at once. The money for the later years is treated as a loan to the charity until such time as it becomes the absolute property of the charity, ie as each successive payment becomes due.

Since 5 April 1991 there is no tax advantage if a wife, not paying tax on her income, makes a covenant in her own name. All covenants in existence at 6 April 1990, including those made by husband and wife, should be reviewed to see whether they are still tax-efficient. This advice applies to joint covenants by husband and wife if one of them is not paying tax on his or her own income.

Companies can also make deeds of covenant in favour of charities.

See also inheritance tax exemptions (page 105) and capital gains tax exemptions (page 89).

## Gift Aid

As from 1 October 1990 an individual can make tax-efficient single gifts to charity. The minimum level is now £250. These gifts are treated as paid net of basic rate income tax, and, as with covenanted payments, the charity will be able to claim repayment of the tax at the basic rate. Under the scheme, the donor will be eligible for relief at the higher rate of income tax, if that applies.

Companies can also take advantage of the scheme, but in the case of a close company (ie a company controlled by its directors, or by five or fewer shareholders) only if the net amount is £250 or more. The paying company will deduct income tax from the payment and account for it to the Inland Revenue. The charity will reclaim the tax and the company will get relief against its profits for the gross amount of the payment.

## Life Assurance Policies

### Qualifying policies

There is tax relief on premiums paid on certain 'qualifying policies' taken out before 14 March 1984. If an earlier contract has been changed after that date so that the benefits or term are increased, it is treated as a new contract.

Qualifying policies must be on the life of the policy holder or spouse and must provide benefit on death. They may also provide other benefits. For instance, an endowment policy may provide for a capital sum after a stated period of at least ten years or on earlier death. The capital sum payable on death, or maturity of the policy, is not taxable.

## Non-qualifying policies

No tax relief is given on premiums on these policies. On maturity the excess of proceeds over premiums paid will be treated as income for the purpose of charging higher rate tax. Credit for basic rate tax on the excess is given when higher rate tax is charged.

A typical non-qualifying policy is a life assurance 'bond' for which a single premium is payable. For some people these bonds can be a very useful form of investment. Amounts up to 5 per cent of the premium can be withdrawn each year and will not be treated as income. At the current rates of interest the ability to withdraw 5 per cent per annum tax free is very attractive, but it is anticipated that these rules will be modified shortly. If nothing is withdrawn in the first year, 10 per cent can be withdrawn in the second year, and so on. If the cumulative total exceeds 5 per cent per year it will later be necessary to calculate by how much it exceeded the premium paid (these details are usually provided by the insurance company but should be carefully checked). If income is lower than average in the year of maturity of the policy, the tax, as well as being deferred, may be lower than the tax would have been on a similarly profitable investment, if income had been assessed throughout. On the other hand, care should be taken to ensure that the surrender does not arise in a year when there is a higher income than normal, because this could mean that more tax would be payable than if income had accrued and been taxed each year. There is a relief available which can reduce this disadvantage. If a person wishes to invest large sums in this type of investment, it is often wise to have a number of separate bonds of different terms rather than one large one.

## Immediate annuities

A person can use capital to buy an annuity. He will pay a sum of money to an insurance company, which will undertake to pay the person a set sum each year throughout his life, and for tax purposes the annual sum (or 'annuity') received will be treated partly as a return of capital (non-taxable) and partly as income which is taxable. The older a person is when he buys such a policy, the larger the annuity will be and also the larger will be the proportion treated as a return of capital. An annuity can be for the remainder of one's life or it can be limited to a shorter period.

## Private Medical Insurance

Tax relief is available in respect of contributions to approved medical insurance schemes, if paid by or on behalf of persons aged 60 or over and the spouses of such people. The insured person (or persons) must be resident in the UK and must have reached the age of 60 before the relevant premium is paid (except that, where the insurance covers a married couple, only one of them needs to have reached the age of 60).

Tax relief is available to the payer of the premium. This might be the insured person or could, for instance, be the son or daughter of the insured, or an employer. Tax at the basic rate may be withheld by the payer. Thus, for instance, while the basic rate remains at 24 per cent the payer will pay only 76 per cent of the premium. Tax relief is limited to 24 per cent only and does not extend to the higher rate of tax.

## Occupational Pension Schemes

A company can contribute towards an approved fund for providing retirement and other benefits for its employees (including directors) and the ordinary annual contributions will be allowable expenses for tax purposes. Additional contributions can also be deducted but, in some cases, the deduction may be spread over a few years. A fund can be limited to certain classes of employees but it is not permitted to discriminate by gender.

There are two main types of approved pension funds:

1. A 'defined benefit scheme' (often called a 'final salary scheme') where the benefits are laid down in the rules.
2. A 'money purchase scheme' where the benefits are dependent on the value of the fund at retirement/death/withdrawal.

The maximum benefits which an approved fund may provide are:

- A pension of two-thirds final pensionable salary.
- A tax-free lump sum on retirement of up to one and a half times final pensionable salary. If this is taken, the amount of pension must be reduced. The lump sum generally cannot exceed £150,000.
- A dependant's pension following death after retirement of up to two-thirds of the employee's unreduced pension.
- A lump sum on death in service of up to four times final salary.
- A dependant's pension on death in service of up to four-ninths final salary.

A fund need not provide all of these benefits and need not go up to the maximum amounts.

On retirement the funds are used to pay the pensions or an annuity is purchased which meets the obligations of the scheme to pay the pension to the member. In 1995 the rules were relaxed to enable the purchase of an annuity to be deferred until the pensioner is aged 75. This enables the pensioner to buy his/her annuity when rates are better, thus increasing the pension income they receive from the annuity. It is the intention that the rules be further relaxed, to enable the individual to take a greater proportion of their pension income at a later date to better fund the increasing costs of care in their old age.

Final salary can be taken as the highest remuneration for any one of the five years preceding death or retirement. Alternatively it can be the average of at least three consecutive years ending in the ten years before death or retirement. If the member is a director who can control at least 20 per cent of the company shares the latter formula must be used.

When making the calculations, it is permissible to take the actual remuneration for any year except the year immediately preceding death or retirement and revalue it in accordance with the movement in the index of retail prices. Thus a person who has been well paid in the past but whose increases in emoluments have not kept pace with inflation may possibly be entitled to a pension of an amount higher than he has ever been paid whilst in service.

Generally, pension provisions are limited to earnings of a prescribed annual amount (see Table 5 on Page 40), but this does not apply to members who joined certain older schemes before 1 June 1989.

In addition to the employer's contribution, the employee may in most cases contribute amounts of up to 15 per cent of his salary and such contributions will be deducted from the amount of income on which he is taxed. Such contributions are known as additional voluntary contributions (AVCs).

An approved fund is exempt from tax on the income generated from the investment of contributions received and is also exempt from capital gains tax. Directors of all close companies are strongly advised to consider whether they should be members of such a fund.

A pension fund must be established by a trust deed which appoints trustees. The trustees may arrange for the day-to-day affairs of the trust to be managed by a life assurance company or by other independent specialists. It is possible for the fund to invest some of its resources in the company (for instance, by purchasing business premises and letting them to the company or by lending money to the company at a commercial rate of interest). In this way, a company which is soundly based, but which may have a poor cash flow, can provide a pension scheme for directors/shareholders without having to find too much immediate cash. Many life assurance companies are prepared to operate schemes in which part of the fund can be reinvested in the company or in assets used by the company and the balance is invested in a wider range of investments.

## *Personal Pension Schemes*

Since 6 April 1988 an employer has not been able to require an employee to be in a company pension scheme. Existing members may opt out if they wish. From 1 July 1988 onwards there has been a scheme for 'personal pensions' which replaced the 'retirement annuity' legislation and includes people who have opted out of employers' pension schemes as well as self-employed people. Those who opted out of their employers' pension arrangements and into a personal pension in the late 1980s should review these arrangements. The pension industry failed in many cases to ensure that the advice given to employees who opted out of company pension schemes in the late 1980s was adequate and the amounts of compensation which will be payable to persons who were ill-advised at that time is significant. To assist in this process of rectification the Chancellor has announced in the 1995 Budget that compensation paid in such cases will be exempt from tax.

Part of an employee's national insurance contributions (see Chapter 4) go towards the State Earnings-related Pension Scheme (SERPS). Employees who have pension arrangements acceptable to the Department of Social Security (DSS) are allowed to contract out of SERPS. The employee and the employer can then pay reduced levels of national insurance.

Personal pensions plans may be more attractive than membership of an employer's scheme to younger people who are likely to change employment several times during their career. For other people, the decision whether to join an employer's scheme, if available, or to have a personal pension plan, and to contract out of SERPS, can be difficult and will be influenced by a lot of different factors such as age and anticipated career development. Every individual is advised to give some consideration to this matter and therefore to have a discussion with a reputable adviser.

Personal pension schemes must be 'money purchase' schemes. This means that the maximum contributions are defined and that the benefits are related to the value of the fund. This contrasts with many employers' pension schemes, where it is the ultimate benefits which are defined and the employers' contributions have to be varied during the life of the scheme to ensure that the fund is able to meet its commitments.

Benefits may start to be taken at any age between 50 and 75 (or even earlier than 50 for a few types of occupation). Up to 25 per cent of the fund may be taken as a lump sum, with a maximum of £150,000.

The maximum contributions (employer and employee combined, where appropriate) are dependent upon the age of the taxpayer and are shown in Tables 4 and 5:

**Table 4** *Contributions to personal pension plans 1989/90–1996/97 by age*

| Age | % of yearly salary |
|---|---|
| Up to 35 | 17½ |
| 36–45 | 20 |
| 46–50 | 25 |
| 51–55 | 30 |
| 56–60 | 35 |
| 61 or more | 40 |

**Table 5** *The maximum incomes on which contributions can be assessed*

| Year | Income |
|---|---|
| 1996/97 | £82,200 |
| 1995/96 | £78,600 |
| 1994/95 | £76,800 |
| 1993/94 | £75,000 |
| 1992/93 | £75,000 |
| 1991/92 | £71,400 |
| 1990/91 | £64,800 |

An employee can choose to have contributions paid in one year treated for tax relief as if paid in the preceding year. In a few exceptional cases they can be 'carried back' a year further and for Lloyd's underwriters two years further. Elections for carry-back must be made within three months of the end of the year of payment. If contributions in any year are less than the permitted maximum, additional contributions can be made within six years.

## *Relief For Interest Paid*

When money is borrowed from a UK bank for the purposes of a business, the interest may be deducted in calculating the taxable trading profit, under the normal business expense rules. This deduction will be available whether the money is borrowed by way of fixed loan or overdraft, but it is essential that the trading entity (ie the sole trader, partnership or company actually carrying on the trade) should be the borrower.

Such normal business expense rules do not help where borrowing is not undertaken for a purpose of trade, profession or vocation or where the person borrowing the money is not the person actually carrying on the business (eg an individual partner borrowing money in connection with the partnership business, or a shareholder borrowing money for the company's business). In such cases it is often still possible for the borrower to obtain tax relief for the interest but it is important to realise that the borrowing must be by way of fixed loan rather than overdraft.

There is no statutory relief where money is borrowed by a partner to purchase land to be used by the partnership, or where a shareholder buys land to be used by a company. If the partner/shareholder actually lets the land to the partnership/company at a commercial rent, then tax relief may be claimed against the rent. In cases where the partnership or company pays interest on behalf of the individual the payment may be treated as a payment of rent. This may affect entitlement to 'retirement relief' from capital gains tax (see page 95).

Table 6 gives a broad summary of the situations where interest can be deducted from income for income tax purposes. It sets out the purposes for which money can be borrowed, the conditions that must be fulfilled and the restrictions that apply.

## Mortgage Interest Relief at Source (MIRAS)

The relief for interest on up to a maximum of £30,000 of the money borrowed to purchase or improve one's home is usually given 'at source'. The value of this tax relief used to be substantial when interest rates were higher and tax relief was given against the payer's highest rate. However, recent years have seen both a reduction in the cost of borrowing and of the tax relief, which fell to 15 per cent in 1995/96.

In a few cases (eg where loans exceed £30,000 or where the lender is not an approved operator of MIRAS), interest is paid in full and the tax inspector gives the tax relief against an assessment for the self-employed or in PAYE coding for employees.

## Rent a Room Relief

Taxpayers can receive up to £3,250 per annum tax free from letting furnished accommodation in their own home, ie their main residence. The sums received can be for rent or for ancillary services, such as meals, laundry etc.

## Vocational Training

Tax relief is available to individuals who pay for their own training that counts towards National Vocational Qualifications or Scottish Vocational training. Tax relief is given by deduction when payment is made at a rate of 24 per cent, even where the individual is not liable to pay income tax. Tax relief at the higher rate has to be claimed from the Inland Revenue.

The relief excludes children under 16 and 16 to 18 year olds in full-time education and recreational activities.

## The Enterprise Investment Scheme (EIS)

The Enterprise Investment Scheme was introduced with effect from 1 January 1994 to replace the Business Expansion Scheme. Together with the Venture Capital Trusts and capital gains reinvestment relief (see page 93) it is designed to encourage the development of new unquoted companies and the enterprise business culture.

Table 6 Borrowings where the interest paid qualifies for income tax relief

| Purpose | Conditions | Restrictions |
| --- | --- | --- |
| Purchase of land or buildings (including caravans, mobile homes and houseboats) in UK or Republic of Ireland (see also p 90) since 5 April 1988. | Property must be:<br>• used as the only or main residence of the borrower; or<br>• acquired by a person living in job-related accommodation and must either be used as a residence or be meant to be used eventually as the only or main residence. | Relief is not allowed on loans of more than £30,000 per residence. However, interest can also be allowed on a bridging loan of up to £30,000 in one year (or even longer in special circumstances), and since 16 March 1993 on loans on former homes provided the house is for sale. |
| Purchase of land or buildings (including caravans, mobile homes and houseboats) in UK or Republic of Ireland. | Money borrowed must be for the purpose of a business in property rental (including furnished and unfurnished lettings). | |
| Business partnership | Money borrowed must buy an interest in a partnership or be lent to a partnership in which the borrower is a member (but not as a limited partner). | No relief on money borrowed to the extent that capital is subsequently recovered from the partnership |
| Business co-operative | Money borrowed must acquire a share in, or be lent to, a co-operative in which the borrower is employed substantially full time. | No relief on money borrowed to the extent that capital is subsequently recovered from the co-operative. |

| Purpose | Conditions | Restrictions |
|---|---|---|
| Shares in a company | Money borrowed must be used to buy close company shares or must be lent to close company for use in its business. The borrower must at the time the interest is paid have at least a 5 per cent interest in the company or be engaged full time in the conduct or management of the company. | If the company is an investment company, no property held by the company must be used as a residence by the individual. No relief on interest up to the amount of any capital subsequently recovered from the company. |
| Shares in employee-controlled company | Money borrowed must be used to acquire shares in an unquoted employee-controlled trading company (within 12 months of its becoming employee-controlled) and the borrower must be a full-time employee. A company is employee-controlled if at least 50 per cent of the shares and of the voting power is owned by full-time employees or their spouses. | If any employee holds over 10 per cent of shares or votes, the excess is deemed to be held by a non-employee. Capital recovered later from the company is deducted from the loan qualifying for tax relief. |
| Purchase of plant and machinery | Money borrowed must be used to buy plant or machinery for use in a business partnership of which the borrower is a partner or, if he is an employee, for use in his employment. | Relief only on interest within three years after the end of tax year in which money borrowed. |
| Purchase of life annuity by person aged 65 or over | At least 90 per cent of money borrowed must be used to buy an annuity for the borrower or for the survivor of the borrower and another person. The loan must be secured on the only or main residence of the annuitant(s). | Relief restricted to interest on £30,000 for individual and joint borrowers. Relief is available for a year (or longer at the Revenue's discretion) after borrower moves out provided property is for sale. |

In order to attract investors, tax relief is given on 20 per cent of investments up to £100,000 per annum. This relief is available where new ordinary shares are issued in an unquoted trading company and the company carries on a trade for a period of at least three years. Up to a half of the amount an individual invests between 6 April and 5 October in a year can be carried back to the previous tax year and income tax relief given subject to a maximum of £15,000.

The sale of shares is exempt from capital gains tax provided the shares are held for at least five years. Where the shares are sold at a loss, relief for the loss can be given against either income tax or capital gains tax.

Where investment is made in an EIS using capital gains proceeds then the combination of reinvestment relief and the EIS relief can give a higher rate taxpayer relief of up to 60 per cent (20 per cent income tax relief and 40 per cent capital gains tax relief).

The scheme encourages investors to bring their experience to the company by allowing the investor to be paid as a director and be eligible for relief provided he was not associated with the enterprise before his shares were issued, which means he and his associates must not hold over 30 per cent of the share capital or be employees.

The company, which must be an unquoted trading company, can only raise £1 million in any year on which tax relief can be given. To qualify, the company must carry on a trading activity which specifically excludes assured tenancies which were so much a feature of the old BES system, and must carry on a trading activity for at least three years.

## *Venture Capital Trusts (VCT)*

The Venture Capital Trusts operate in tax terms much like the Enterprise Investment Scheme. However, as an investment it is entirely different. Under the Enterprise Investment Scheme an investor has a direct stake in an unquoted trading company and can be involved in its management. A Venture Capital Trust must be quoted on the Stock Exchange and operates much in the same manner, as well as enjoying the same corporation tax exemption on capital gains, as an investment trust. The Venture Capital Trust will be professionally run. The Trust will itself hold shares in unquoted trading companies. An investor thus holds shares in the Venture Capital Trust and does not hold any direct investment in the underlying unquoted trading companies.

A Venture Capital Trust must have at least 70 per cent of its investments in unquoted trading companies with no more than 15 per cent in any one company or group of companies. At least 30 per cent of the investment in unquoted companies must be in ordinary shares carrying no preferential rights. Only investments up to £1 million count towards the 70 per cent investment test.

A Venture Capital Trust will hold a variety of investments in a number of different unquoted trading companies and thus the risk to the investor is spread. Furthermore, an investment in an unquoted company which becomes quoted counts as an unquoted company for the purposes of the investment test. However, as the investor has no direct investment in the underlying private trading companies he must rely upon the managers of the Venture Capital Trust. Investors will need to choose a Venture Capital Trust where the managers have experience in this specialised commercial area.

The investor in Venture Capital Trusts may invest up to £100,000 per annum and be exempt from income tax on dividends and capital gains tax on sale of those investments. The investor will also be entitled to 20 per cent income tax relief on investments of up to £100,000 per annum, provided that the shares in the Venture Capital Trusts are held for five years.

Like the rules of the Enterprise Investment Scheme, the Venture Capital Trust can also be used as a medium whereby the capital gain on the disposal of any asset can be held over. Thus it is possible for the higher rate taxpayer to obtain tax relief of up to 60 per cent (20 per cent income tax relief and 40 per cent capital gains tax postponement).

To date there have only been a handful of such trusts launched. It remains to be seen whether these new Venture Capital Trusts will prove as popular as the old BES.

## The Business Expansion Scheme (BES)

The 'business expansion scheme' was withdrawn from 31 December 1993. It had served its purpose and has been replaced by the new 'Enterprise Investment Scheme'. For investors and companies who have benefited from the scheme, care must be taken during the life of the individual scheme, which runs for five years from time of investment, to ensure that the tax relief is not withdrawn and the tax benefits reclaimed by the Inland Revenue from the investor.

### *Shares disposed of within five years*

If shares are sold all the relief will be withdrawn. If they are not sold at arm's length and the money or other value received for them is less than their cost, the relief will be withdrawn up to the amount received. If the value received exceeds cost, all the relief will be withdrawn. On withdrawal, tax for the year in which relief was given is recalculated, but, for the purpose of charging interest, the relevant date is the date of the disposal which caused the withdrawal.

### *Shares disposed of after five years*

Shares issued after 18 March 1986 on which relief is given and not withdrawn shall not give rise to any chargeable gain or allowable loss on disposal by the person who received the relief.

If a person has some shares in a company on which relief has been claimed and also has other shares in the company, there are special rules to identify each category for capital gains tax purposes.

The rules that apply to BES companies are complex. Relief for shares issued on or after 16 March 1993 will be refused or withdrawn if the investor or any associate borrows money from any source within two years before, or five years after, making the investment and the loan is in any way linked to the making of the investment.

## Other events causing withdrawal of relief

Relief is withdrawn if within five years the individual receives value from the company. This can happen for instance if:

- he borrows from the company
- the company transfers an asset to him at less than full worth
- it repays or redeems any capital or makes a payment for giving up any rights
- it repays any debt it had to him before the shares were issued.

Relief is also withdrawn if, within five years, the company ceases to carry on a qualifying trade; or if the claimant becomes connected with the company; or if the company otherwise becomes ineligible. If any event does occur which requires relief to be withdrawn, the law requires the claimant to notify the tax inspector within 60 days.

## Tax Payment Dates and Interest

### Interest on Repayments ('Repayment Supplement')

Up to 1995/96 if the Inland Revenue makes a repayment of tax to a person more than twelve months after the end of the fiscal year for which it was paid, and if the person was resident in the UK for that year, it will pay repayment supplement in addition to the tax. It is calculated from the end of the year following the year of assessment until the end of the tax month (ie a month ending on the 5th) in which the tax is repaid. See Table 8 for rates in recent years.

If the tax had not been paid by the person within twelve months of the year of assessment, the supplement only begins to run at the end of the fiscal year in which the tax was paid.

Repayment Supplement is not treated as income for taxation purposes.

Similar provisions apply for companies, but the minimum level on which Repayment Supplement is paid is £100. For companies, supplement is calculated by reference to the date on which corporation tax (see Chapter 5) for the relevant period would normally be due. If the tax was paid within twelve months of that date, supplement begins to run on the first anniversary of the date. If the tax was paid later, supplement begins to run on the anniversary of the date following the date of payment.

## From 1996/97

Under Self Assessment the Inland Revenue will make a payment of repayment supplement on overpaid tax and Class IV NIC from the due date or, if later, the day of payment, to the date the repayment is made.

Now that the Inland Revenue has computerised much of its collection process it is able to calculate interest on a daily basis and consequently there is no minimum level at which repayment supplement is not paid.

## Due Dates for Payment

Income is divided into a number of different types known as 'schedules' (Table 9 explains these in more detail). Up to 1995/96 tax on different types of income was payable at different times. Income received after deduction of tax at basic rate is still categorised to determine the type of income to find when tax should be paid. Table 7 shows the different schedules and their due dates. 1995/96 is the last year of Inland Revenue assessment.

From 1996/97 a uniform set of dates for the payment of income tax and capital gains tax starting from 31 January 1997 applies (see Table 7). The 1995/96 assessments on the schedular system will determine the two payments on account due for the 1996/97 transitional year.

## Interest on Overdue Tax

Up to 1995/96 if tax is not paid on the due date, interest becomes chargeable. The rate of interest is currently the same as for repayment supplement (see Table 8). The interest paid cannot be regarded as a deductible expense.

If an appeal is made against an assessment and the appellant has reason to believe that the tax charge is overstated, he may ask that collection of the excess be postponed. If this request is granted, collection can be delayed until the appeal is settled but, if settlement is delayed (see below) beyond six months after the due date, interest will be charged from the end of the six-month period. The six months' grace does not apply to the second instalment of tax on trades, professions or vocations: interest may run immediately from the due date.

If an assessment is made late, the due date becomes 30 days after the assessment rather than the normal due date. The period of postponement free of interest can only run to six months after the normal due date.

When an appeal is made which might take a long time to resolve, the appellant must consider whether he should withhold payment of the amount in dispute and risk being charged with interest if he should lose his appeal, or whether he should pay the tax and then reclaim it if he wins his appeal.

## Table 7  Income schedules and due dates

| Type of income | Date of payment 1995/96 | Date of payment 1996/97 |
|---|---|---|
| Schedule D<br>Cases I and II<br>Trades, professions or vocations<br>assessed Case V | 50% 1 Jan 1996<br><br>50% 1 July 1996 | **<br>50% 31 Jan 1997<br><br>50% 31 July 1997 |
| Schedule A<br>Schedule D<br>Cases III and VI<br>Cases IV and V assessments other than<br>trades, professions or vocations | *<br><br>1 Jan 1996 | **<br><br>31 Jan 1997 |
| Higher rate tax on any income from<br>which basic rate tax has been deducted<br>at source or which carries a tax credit | 31 Dec 1996 | **<br>31 Jan 1998 |
| Schedule E remuneration from<br>employment | PAYE | PAYE |

\* 1995/96 Schedule A tax is due on 1 January, but the amount of income to be assessed cannot be known until after the following 5 April. To get round this difficulty the law provides that the tax inspector shall make the assessment on the same amount as the final assessment for the previous year. The tax on this assessment is payable on 1 January, but the assessment is then reviewed after 5 April and revised to statements prepared on an accounting, accruals, basis.

\*\* For 1996/97 these payments on account under transitional payment arrangement, before Self Assessment is fully operational, will be based on the 1995/96 liability. The 31 January 1998 will be a balancing payment to clear 1996/97 liability.

The 1995/96 assessment at the 1996/97 instalment payment can be reduced if the source of income ceases (eg if the property has been sold).

For revised assessments, any increased amount of tax is regarded as due at the date applicable to the original assessment, and interest will be calculated on that basis.

The Inland Revenue also has the power to charge interest for a period before an assessment was made, if the reason for its being made late was negligence (or worse) on the part of the taxpayer.

If tax is not paid on the due date, interest becomes chargeable and calculated from the due date to the date of payment. If tax remains outstanding after 28 days, a surcharge of 5 per cent is added to the unpaid amount. A further surcharge of 5 per cent is added on amounts still outstanding after six months.

Under Self Assessment the initial two instalments are based on the previous year's tax liabilities. These instalments cannot be increased but may be reduced on a claim being made before 31 January following the end of the tax year. To curtail abuses of this system where unjustified claims are made to reduce initial instalments, penalties will be charged. The penalty will be equal to the difference between the amount that should have been paid and the payments on account.

The penalties may be reduced by the Inland Revenue, or on appeal, amended or cancelled by the Commissioners.

## Rates of Interest

The rates of interest in recent years for the repayment supplement and unpaid tax are shown in Table 8. The rates apply to both income tax and capital gains tax.

Table 8  *Rates of interest for the repayment supplement and on overdue tax*

| Date | % |
|---|---|
| 6/11/90–5/03/91 | 12.25 |
| 6/03/91–5/05/91 | 11.5 |
| 6/05/91–5/07/91 | 10.75 |
| 6/07/91–5/10/91 | 10.0 |
| 6/10/91–5/11/92 | 9.25 |
| 6/11/92–5/12/92 | 7.75 |
| 6/12/92–5/03/93 | 7.0 |
| 6/03/93–5/01/94 | 6.25 |
| 6/01/94–5/10/94 | 5.5 |
| 6/10/94–5/03/95 | 6.25 |
| 6/03/95–5/02/96 | 7.0 |
| 6/02/96 onwards | 6.25 |

## Certificates of Tax Deposit

A person can make advance provision for tax which will be payable in the future by buying 'certificates of tax deposit'. The minimum deposit is £2,000 which may be deposited with any tax collector. Additional deposits are in multiples of £500. Deposits of £100,000 or more must be sent direct to the Bank of England. The certificates can be used in payment of:

- income tax (other than PAYE or the money which must be deducted from certain payments to sub-contractors in the construction industry)
- corporation tax (only with certificates purchased before 1 October 1993)
- capital gains tax, or
- inheritance tax.

Deposits earn interest from the date of deposit to the date they are used in settlement of tax or to an earlier 'normal due date', but subject to a maximum of six years. For the first two years it is the rate prevailing on the date of deposit. For the next two years it is the rate prevailing on the second anniversary and for the next two it is the rate prevailing on the fourth anniversary. The rates of interest are set by the Inland Revenue. Deposits can be withdrawn instead of being used to pay tax, but in that case a lower rate of interest is payable. The interest receivable is taxable.

## Types of Income

Each source of income is classified under a heading known as a schedule

## Table 9 The bases on which various types of income are assessed

| Schedule | Type of Income | Basis of Assessment |
|---|---|---|
| A | Rents and other income from property (except from mines, quarries, etc). From 6 April 1996 this includes furnished and unfurnished lettings. | See page 54. |
| C | This has been abolished with effect from 1996/97. | |
| D (Case I) | Trading income (except if carried on wholly abroad). Farming income, income from mines, quarries, etc. | See page 66. |
| D (Case II) | Income from professions and vocations (except if carried on wholly abroad). | See page 66. |
| D (Case III) | Interest, annuities and annual payments from which tax is not deducted at source. | Actual income of the current year. |
| D (Case IV) | Income from securities outside UK. | See page 53. |
| D (Case V) | Income from possessions outside UK. Income from trades, professions or work carried on wholly abroad. Foreign pensions. | See page 53. |
| D Case (VI) | All income not included under any other case or schedule. | Profits arising in the year of assessment. |
| E | Emoluments from offices or employments. UK pensions. | See page 55. |
| F | Dividends and certain other distributions from UK companies. | Tax credit for lower rate where applicable. Assessed on amount received in the year plus tax credit. |
| Other income | Bank and building society interest paid net. | Higher rate, where applicable, assessed on amount received in the year 'grossed up' to include the credit for lower rate tax. |

and tax under different schedules is assessed in different ways. Under the new Self Assessment regulations which start on 6 April 1996 the method of assessing income is being simplified. The current schedules classification, however, remains although it has little relevance to today. The most common form of income, for instance, is that received by way of salary, wages and bonuses from employment. This is taxed under Schedule E through the pay as you earn (PAYE) system where the income is subject to tax as it arises. The self-employed on the other hand pay income tax under Schedule D Case I and Schedule D Case II. Under the new Self Assessment regulations income tax will be assessed on the income of the year. This is called the current year basis. There are transitional arrangements covering the period immediately prior to the introduction of Self Assessment but these are complex. Table 9 details the schedules and the current bases of assessment but excludes the transitional arrangements.

## Domicile, Residence and Ordinary Residence

Where income arises or is earned abroad, the amount assessable may be determined by reference to the amount remitted to the UK rather than the amount arising (see page 54). The 'domicile', 'residence' and 'ordinary residence' of the individual will be relevant in deciding whether the 'arising' basis or the 'remittance' basis applies. The meaning of these expressions is not easy to define and it is advisable to obtain professional guidance in any case of doubt but the following paragraphs give a broad idea of the differences in meaning.

### Domicile

Domicile is something which applies to a person substantially for all of his life. It refers to where he has his roots and, although it is possible to change domicile, many people who move around the world do not do so. For a person who was not born in the UK and whose parents were not UK nationals it is unlikely that he will be regarded as domiciled here unless he has taken very positive steps to indicate that he intends to stay here for the rest of his life and to sever his links with his previous country. Even if he has taken such steps, he may not have changed his domicile. Conversely, a person whose roots and birth were in this country will probably still be domiciled here even if he has been abroad for long periods, unless he has taken conscious and positive steps to change his domicile (see also page 115).

### Residence

Residence is quite a different concept. For each tax year a decision has to be made as to whether a person is resident. It is possible to be resident in more than one country for the same year and so a person cannot say that he is not resident in the UK for any particular year merely because he is resident elsewhere.

If a person spends 183 or more days of the tax year in this country he will be regarded as resident for that year. Days of arrival and departure are normally ignored.

If less than 183 days are spent here, he may still be treated as resident for the year, if it is one of a series during which he makes regular and substantial visits to this country. Visits averaging three months or more for four consecutive years will be regarded as both substantial and regular. They may be so regarded even for the first year if it is apparent at the outset that the pattern will be continued.

## Ordinary residence

Ordinarily resident means habitually resident. Thus a person who has been resident here for many years, but who goes abroad for a period which includes a full tax year, may be 'ordinarily resident' for the year of absence even if not 'resident'. On the other hand, a person can be resident for a year without being ordinarily resident.

## Concessions

Although residence and ordinary residence should be determined for a whole tax year, there are circumstances when the Inland Revenue will treat different periods of a tax year as if they were different years and consider the position for each period separately. This treatment will be accorded in many cases:

- when a person first comes to this country as a permanent resident;
- when a person leaves for a permanent residence abroad; or
- when a person first takes up full-time employment abroad.

## Income tax

Income tax is normally chargeable on all income arising in the UK whether the person to whom it arises is resident here or not. However, there are some Government securities on which tax is not charged unless the holder is ordinarily resident in the UK. For income which arises abroad, see page 53.

## Inheritance tax

Inheritance tax applies to transfers of all property situated in the UK or abroad if the transferor is domiciled in the UK. If the transferor is domiciled outside the UK, the tax only applies to transfers of property in the UK.

## Capital gains tax

Capital gains tax is chargeable on gains arising to anybody who is resident or ordinarily resident in the UK for the year in which the gain arises, regardless of whether the asset which gave rise to the gain is situated in the UK or elsewhere. However, a person who is not domiciled in the UK will only be assessed on gains arising abroad to the extent that they are remitted to this country.

A person who is not resident or ordinarily resident in the UK may be assessed on gains arising in the UK if he carries on a trade through a branch or agency here and the gain arises on the disposal of an asset which was used for that trade.

## Double taxation relief

Sometimes income may be taxed in two countries. This may happen, for instance, if a person is resident in one country but has income arising in another. Agreements have therefore been made with many countries to help reduce the impact of this double taxation. The nature of the relief will depend upon the type of income taxable and it may also vary from country to country.

Double taxation relief normally applies to capital gains tax and corporation tax as well as to income tax. The UK has also made agreements with some countries in connection with inheritance tax but these are rather fewer in number.

In some cases, income is taxed in both countries but one country allows a credit for the tax in the other. The general result of such credits is that the tax suffered is restricted to the higher of the two rates involved.

If a person resident in the UK has income which arises and is taxed in a foreign country with which there is no agreement, some relief from UK tax will generally be given in respect of that foreign tax.

## Income from Abroad (Schedule D, Cases IV and V)

Table 10 shows how income from abroad is assessed. 'R' means that only the remittance to this country is assessed, '100' means 100 per cent is assessed, '90' means 90 per cent.

Under the new rules introduced with Self Assessment, income from abroad is assessed on the current year basis (ie income arising in the year of assessment) from 1994/95 onwards. However, there are complicated transitional rules covering 1995/96 and 1996/97.

## Schedule A

This schedule applies to all property income. With effect from 1995/96 the rules have been changed and this schedule now taxes the profits on gains arising from any business of renting or letting of land and buildings. This will include licence fees to occupy land, rent, furnished and unfurnished letting. It does not include profits or gains from woodlands under commercial management, farming or market gardening where the profits are charged under Schedule D Case I, or mineral rights and royalties. Furnished holiday lettings, previously assessed under Schedule D Case VI, are now brought within Schedule A for income tax purposes.

The profit/loss is computed in the same way as for a business under Schedule D Case I (see page 66). Loan interest incurred wholly and exclusively for the purpose of the letting businesses is deductible under the normal rules. However, although Schedule A income is computed in the same way as a trade, it is still investment income for other purposes.

Landlords with a gross income from property under £15,000 need only state the gross income, total expenses and net profit on their tax returns.

Table 10 *The assessment of income from abroad*

| Status of taxpayer | | | | Trade, profession or vocation | Pension | Income from securities, possessions |
|---|---|---|---|---|---|---|
| **Person resident in UK** | Domiciled in UK | British (or Irish) subject | Ordinarily resident in UK | 100 | 90 | 100 |
| | | | Not ordinarily resident in UK | R | R | R |
| | | Not British subject | | 100 | 90 | 100 |
| | Not domiciled in UK | | | R | R | R |
| **Person not resident in UK** | | | | No liability | No liability | No liability |

## Premiums on Leases

A premium is an amount paid in connection with a new leasehold interest. Thus, if a lessee sells the residue of a lease, the capital sum received is not a premium. If he creates a sub-lease for a capital sum, that capital sum is a premium.

A premium receivable for a lease of up to fifty years is taxable as income under Schedule A. If the lease is for a period of two years or more, the assessment is on the premium less a reduction of 2 per cent for every complete year except the first. Thus, on a fifty-year lease with 20 years left to run, the assessment will be on 62 per cent of the premium.

If a tenant is required to make improvements to the property, the value of those improvements is treated as if it were a premium received. Certain other receipts are also treated as premiums. These include sums paid instead of rents, payments for variation or waiver of the terms of a lease, and payments for the assignments of leases originally granted at an under-value.

Where premises are occupied for business purposes, the amount of premium (or other payment) treated as income of the landlord can also be treated as additional rent payable by the tenant. The figure is treated as spread over the period of the lease. For instance, in the above example, where 62 per cent of the premium for a twenty-year lease is assessed, an amount equal to 3.1 per cent of the premium could be treated as an additional deductible business expense in each of the twenty years by the tenant.

## Furnished Holiday Lettings

Furnished holiday lettings are now taxed under Schedule A for income tax but the income is treated as earned income for the purposes of losses and personal pensions (see page 37). In addition the 'rollover relief' for replacement of business assets is available for capital gains tax. So also is 'retirement relief' (see page 95).

## Schedule E

Under Schedule E tax is charged on the emoluments from any office (eg a directorship) or employment. The word 'emoluments' includes perquisites – 'perks' – and all kinds of profits, as well as such obvious remuneration as wages, salaries, fees, commissions, etc. (See page 57). Emoluments arising from the employment can be assessed even if, like tips for instance, they do not come from the employer. Deductions can be claimed for travelling expenses incurred in the performance of duties and also for other expenses incurred wholly, exclusively and necessarily in the performance of the duties of the office or employment.

In some circumstances where remuneration is earned abroad, the assessment is based on the amount remitted to this country rather than on the amount received.

## Payments on retirement or removal

Tax under Schedule E is chargeable on some payments on leaving – usually where they are stipulated as part of the terms of the employment. If the payment is in connection with the death, injury or disability of the employee it will be exempt. In other cases the first £30,000 is exempt.

Compensation or other payments on termination have not normally been within the meaning of 'emolument' but have been taxed by special legislation. Since 1 November 1991 most ex-gratia payments made on death or retirement have been subject to tax under Schedule E, unless specific approval is sought to make the payment part of a cash lump-sum pension payment on retirement or in accordance with the pension regulations.

## Redundancy payments and schemes

Statutory redundancy payments are exempt from tax. Non-statutory payments may strictly be taxable if they can be construed as part of the terms of employment or if there is an expectation of them. In practice the Inland Revenue will not want to tax them if it is convinced that they are to meet genuine cases of redundancy and are not merely terminal bonuses. Employers may discuss proposed payments or schemes in advance with inspectors to ascertain whether they fall within the Revenue practice. Broadly the criteria looked for by the inspector are:

1. Payments are only made on account of genuine redundancy.
2. The employee has been continuously employed for a least two years.
3. The payments are not made to selected employees only.
4. The payments are not excessively large in relation to earnings and length of service.

## Profit-related Pay

An employer can set up a scheme under which part of his employees' pay is profit-related. If this scheme is approved by the Board of Inland Revenue, some of the profit-related pay can be exempt from income tax. It has to be said that the law in this area is complex and this mitigates against the obvious economic advantages of having a workforce whose remuneration is at least in part reflected in the economic achievements of their employer. None the less, an increasing number of people are now benefiting from profit-related pay and the consequent reduced levels of tax bills.

The maximum exempt figure in a tax year for each individual is the lower of:

- £4,000, or
- 20 per cent of total pay for the profit-related pay accounting period (including profit-related pay).

If an employer wishes to introduce a scheme, he must decide the accounting period from which he wants it to start and apply for registration not more than six months before that date. The scheme may be for all employees or it can be limited to those in an 'employment unit'. If an employment unit is less than the whole of the trade, it must be possible to provide audited profit figures for the unit, separately from the rest of the undertaking. With effect from 1 December 1993 the rules were tightened to prevent certain abuses of the system.

No person who controls more than 25 per cent of the company's share capital (either on his own or in conjunction with any associates) can be a participator in such a scheme.

An employer can leave out of the scheme anybody whose hours are less than 20 per week and anybody who has only short service with the employer. (The employer can decide what is meant by short service, up to a maximum of three years).

The scheme must be such that at least 80 per cent of the employees in the relevant employment unit are included in it but, in calculating the 80 per cent, the employer can disregard:

- people who are not eligible under the 25 per cent shareholding rule;
- part-timers who are excluded; and
- people who are excluded because of short service.

After every profit period (normally one year) for which the scheme operates, the employer must send to the Board of the Inland Revenue a return and a report by an independent accountant certifying that the terms of the scheme have been complied with.

## *Benefits in Kind*

In addition to payment in money an employed person will be assessed on other emoluments arising because of employment. These are called 'benefits in kind'. Types of emolument assessable are:

1. Vouchers for cash, goods or services.
2. Provision of anything which is convertible into money. Assessed on resale value.
3. Settlement of a personal debt or liability incurred by the employee.
4. Provision of living accommodation (but not where it is necessary for the job or where there is a special security risk or where it is desirable and customary in that type of occupation). On homes under £75,000 it is the annual value less any rent paid which is assessed. Above this value it is the annual value of the home plus a

prescribed percentage (see Table 11) of the excess of the capital value over £75,000 which is assessed. If the property was acquired by the employer more than six years before occupation by the employee, the cost is deemed to be the market value at the date of first occupation.
5. Vans made available by the employer for private use will be assessed at £500 per annum (£350 per annum if over four years old).

## *Other Emoluments*

Employees who earn £8,500 or over in a year, and company directors (but not full-time directors who have less than a 5 per cent interest in the company, unless earning over £8,500) may also be assessed on a wider range of emoluments. In deciding whether a person's emoluments exceed £8,500 all the items listed below (as well as those listed above) are taken into account. The wider range of emoluments comprises:

- Cars which are available for private use. See Table 12.
- The cost of provision of a chauffeur.
- Beneficial loans of up to £5,000 to an individual are exempt from tax as from 6 April 1994. Where loans are for more than £5,000, the old rules apply to the excess over £5,000, and the assessment is by reference to the difference between interest paid by the employee and interest at a prescribed rate. If the employee had paid a full rate of interest, relief would have been claimable under any of the circumstances described in Table 6, no assessment will be made. The prescribed rates for recent years are set out in Table 11.

  Rules are to be introduced to restrict the tax relief on home loans from employers so that the relief is identical to that available under MIRAS (see page 41) thereby restricting tax relief to 15 per cent from 1995/96.
- Loans written off. The amount written off is treated as remuneration unless it is written off following the death of the employee.
- Expenses connected with living accommodation. If the occupation is:
  — necessary for the job, or
  — because of a special security risk, or
  — desirable and customary in the particular occupation

  the assessment to cover heat, light, cleaning, repairs and use of furniture will not exceed 10 per cent of the emoluments (after deducting any expenses, capital allowances and pension contributions). From 6 April 1989 certain expenses on security for people who, because of their occupation, face threats from terrorists etc are not taxable as benefits.
- Other assets made available for the use of the employee. The assessment is on 20 per cent of the original value less any rent paid if the asset was first provided after 5 April 1980.

- Assets given to the employee. For assets first made available after 5 April 1980, assessment will be on the market value at the first time made available less any amounts already assessed as benefit.
- The acquisition of shares at an undervalue (other than under an approved profit-sharing scheme).
- Medical insurance (eg BUPA). The assessment is based on the cost to the employer. No assessment is made on premiums to cover travel abroad on business.
- Scholarship income. If a scholarship, bursary or similar endowment is paid to a member of the family of an employee by reason of his employment, the employee may be assessed. There are exceptions where over 75 per cent of the payments made by the scholarship fund cover children of people who are not employees.
- Mobile telephones — £200.
- In-house benefits. Where an employee obtains free or discounted goods or services, which are normally generated or sold by his employer, unless there is a specific valuation rule (as for motor cars and mobile telephones), assessment will be based only on the marginal cost to the employer. School teachers and public transport employees are particularly likely to benefit from this major change in interpretation of the law. There is an exemption from tax for the provision of in-house sports and recreational facilities to an employee.
- Other benefits provided for the employee. The assessment is on the cash equivalent.

In addition to the above, a director or employee earning over £8,500 may be assessed on all expenses paid to or for him. He will be entitled to claim a deduction for travelling expenses necessarily incurred in the performance of his duties and also for other expenses incurred wholly, exclusively and necessarily in the performance of his duties. If he has been assessed on the provision of a chauffeur's services, he may claim a deduction for the part of those services attributable to necessary business journeys.

Table 11 *Prescribed rates of interest for assessing benefits in kind and beneficial loans*

| Dates | % |
|---|---|
| 6/10/91–5/03/92 | 11.25 |
| 6/03/92–5/06/92 | 10.75 |
| 6/06/92–5/11/92 | 10.5 |
| 6/11/92–5/12/92 | 9.75 |
| 6/12/92–5/01/93 | 9.0 |
| 6/01/93–5/03/93 | 8.25 |
| 6/03/93–5/01/94 | 7.75 |
| 6/01/94–5/11/94 | 7.50 |
| 6/11/94–5/10/95 | 8.0 |
| 6/10/95— | 7.75 |

## Company Cars

If you have a company car you use privately, you are assessed for an amount of income that is dependent upon the period of use and value of the car, the age of the car, the business mileage and whether the company pays for petrol. The petrol is assessed by a 'fuel scale charge'. From 6 April 1994 the assessable benefit of the car is based on the original list price of the car (including all accessories) with discounts for mileage and age. For cars over 15 years old and worth more than £15,000, market value is used if this is more than cost. The benefit on which the employee is assessed is 35 per cent of the list price (or value) of the car, with a discount of a third for more than 2,500 business miles or two-thirds for more than 18,000 business miles. The resulting figure is discounted by a third if the car is over four years old, to arrive at the figure on which tax is paid. The list price is used rather than the cost of the car and the list price also includes the cost of accessories, with the exception of those relating to modification for the disabled. The charges applicable are added to income and assessed under Schedule E, generally through the PAYE system. Table 12 gives the fuel scale charges. Table 13 gives the basis of assessing the car benefit. There will be no addition for fuel if the employee pays for all fuel used for private purposes. See also page 76 on the use of private cars.

Table 12  *Fuel scale charges (£) (1995/96 and 1996/97)*

| Fuel | Engine size | 1995/96 | 1996/97 |
|---|---|---|---|
| **Petrol** | Up to 1400cc | 670 | 710 |
| **Petrol** | 1,401 to 2,000 | 850 | 890 |
| **Petrol** | 2,001 and over | 1,260 | 1,320 |
| **Diesel** | Up to 2,000 | 605 | 640 |
| **Diesel** | 2,001 and over | 780 | 820 |

Table 13  *Employee car and van benefits*

**Cars**

> **Benefit = Original list price × 35%**
>
> Benefit reduced by
> - ¹/₃, if business mileage is between 2,501 and 17,999 miles per year
> - ²/₃, if business mileage is 18,000 miles or more
>
> and is further reduced by
> - ¹/₃, where car is four years old or more
>
> Original list price is manufacturer's price (when the car was registered) plus price of accessories, subject to overall limit of £80,000. If the car is over 15 years old and the market value greater than £15,000, market value can be substituted.

**Vans**

| | Vans under 4 years old | Vans 4 years old or more |
|---|---|---|
| Vans less than 3.5 tonnes in weight | £500 | £350 |

## Share Schemes

### Savings-related Share Option Schemes (SAYEs)

A company may run a scheme which gives employees an option to buy shares in the company at some future date (normally just over three years, five years or just over seven years ahead) but at a predetermined price and which assists them to save money monthly to do this.

All full-time employees with over five years' service must be given the right to join the scheme. Other employees may be included at the discretion of the company.

The shares must be ordinary shares with no restrictions. The purchase price of the shares must be not less than 80 per cent of the value of ordinary shares at the date the option is granted.

The employee will save a regular amount each month which need not exceed £5 and must not exceed £250 for the given period. The savings must be under a special contract (SAYE) with the Department of National Savings or a building society. The savings are deducted monthly from pay by the employer.

The contracts earn a tax-free bonus at the end of the scheme period (after three, five or seven years) and a further tax-free bonus after two years if repayment is not claimed during the last two years. The accumulated fund is then used to buy shares under the option agreement and the fact that these are normally more valuable than the amount paid does not give rise to an income tax charge. The price paid is the basis for the calculation of any future capital gain.

### Non-savings-related Share Option Schemes

A company may apply for approval to operate a share option scheme under which directors and employees are given the future right to acquire shares at the value of those shares when the option is granted. There used to be special rules that applied to the profits arising from the exercise of these options that enabled the profit to be assessable to capital gains tax. However, due to certain abuses, this was changed in 1995 so that in future all such profits are taxable as income tax.

A new relief was introduced from 17 July 1995 which will enable companies to grant options worth up to £20,000 to each employee. If the option granted is approved by the Inland Revenue no income tax will be payable either when the option is granted or exercised. The £20,000 limit is set by reference to the value of the shares at the time the option is granted.

### Approved Profit-sharing Schemes

A company may pay money to trustees to buy shares in the company for the benefit of employees. If this is done via an approved scheme, the company can deduct the money and the trustees' necessary expenses in calculating its liability to corporation tax.

The shares must be ordinary shares and must be held by trustees on behalf of the individual employees. The shares must not be capable of being withdrawn within two years, except in the event of the death of the employee for whom they are held.

Every full-time employee with five years' or more service must be included. Other employees may be included at the discretion of the company. The value of shares acquired in 1991/92 or in later years for an employee earning under £30,000 must not exceed £3,000. For a more highly paid person the value must not exceed 10 per cent of earnings, with a maximum of £8,000.

Employees are not taxed on the value of the shares provided for them. If they are held for over three years they can be sold and no income tax will be chargeable. If they are sold within three years they are taxable in full.

If an employee leaves because he has reached retirement age or because of redundancy or disability and sells the shares within three years, income tax is payable but is limited to tax on 50 per cent of the value at acquisition date (or, if lower, 50 per cent of sale proceeds).

The shares are within the scope of capital gains tax, with the value at the time of acquisition being treated as the cost.

## Employee Share Ownership Plans (ESOPs)

A further type of employee participation scheme, which goes further than approved profit-sharing schemes, is available. Companies can contribute money to ESOP trusts and obtain corporation tax relief on the contribution. Trusts must use the money within nine months to subscribe for new shares (or buy existing shares) in the company, can borrow money for such acquisitions, and can use contributions from the employing company to fund such borrowing.

A majority of trustees must be employees who have never had more than a 5 per cent holding in the company. At least one trustee must be a solicitor or member of an appropriate professional body.

Beneficiaries must exclude all employees or directors who have (or recently had) a material interest. They must include all other employees who have been employed five years or more and who work 20 or more hours per week. Other employees who work 20 or more hours but have worked for less than five years may be included.

Shares acquired must be distributed to beneficiaries within seven years of acquisition.

A special rollover relief (see page 93) may be available to a shareholder disposing of shares to an ESOP where a replacement asset is acquired within six months of the disposal.

## Anti-Avoidance Laws

These are laws under which the income of one person can be deemed, for tax purposes, to be the income of another person or under which capital receipts can be taxed as income. The most important provisions are:

1. Taxation of certain capital gains on land and buildings as income.
2. Income arising to a person abroad being attributed to a UK resident in certain cases.
3. Profits on certain shares and securities being treated as income if the transactions cannot be shown to be carried out for bona fide commercial reasons.
4. Dividends and interest being attributed to a person other than the person who receives them where shares or securities have changed ownership in certain circumstances.
5. Capital arising to an individual from a sale, or income earned, to be taxed as income.

In addition, judicial interpretation of the law makes it clear that in some circumstances where a series of transactions takes place for tax avoidance purposes, the substance of transactions can be taxed without limitation by the form in which they were carried out.

# 3

# Business Tax

Overview — Profits — Adjustments to Profit — Capital Expenditure — Income tax of Trades, Professions and Vocations for Partnerships and Sole Traders — Sub-contractors in the Construction Industry — Farming and Agricultural Profit — Commercial Woodlands — Capital Allowances — Business Economic Notes

## Overview

Any business will pay tax on the profits of that business. The business profits of a company are subject to corporation tax (see Chapter 5) while the profits of a partnership or sole trader are subject to income tax (see Trades, Professions and Vocations below).

## Profits

The profit (or loss) of a business is not easy to define. The accounts of the business will show the profitability of the business. However, the profits that are taxable will be differently computed. Profit has to be divided between capital and income profits. Income profits are normally calculated by eliminating the capital profit. Capital profits are taxed in accordance with the rules of capital gains tax (see Chapter 6). In a company the taxable capital gain is added to the taxable income and the total thereof is subject to tax at the appropriate rate of corporation tax. For a partnership or sole trader the taxable capital gain is also taxed in accordance with the rules of capital gains tax. However, where the gain relates to a partnership asset, it is apportioned amongst the partners each of whom is taxed at the rate calculated as if this were an addition to his income which is subject to income tax.

The profit of a business is measured over a defined accounting period. The profit will be arrived at by aggregating all the income due in the period and deducting the allowable expenses payable. In general the normal accounting rules properly utilised in the preparation of annual accounts will be acceptable in arriving at the income and expenditure of the accounting period. For expenditure to be allowable as a deduction it must be expended in the furtherance of the trade and be wholly and exclusively for the trade. This means that certain expenditure such as entertaining expenditure or private expenditure of the proprietor cannot be deducted.

There are special rules for capital expenditure whereby, instead of permitting the deduction of the depreciation charged in the accounts a deduction for 'capital allowances' is allowed in lieu.

Interest payable (except for bank interest) and pension premiums payable are only allowed as a deduction if they are paid within the accounting period. All remuneration charged in the accounts can only be deducted provided it is paid within nine months of the end of the accounting period.

## Adjustments to Profit

To arrive at taxable income, the following would be added to the profit in the accounts:

- Depreciation of fixed assets
- Entertaining expenditure
- Private expenditure
- Capital expenditure (including related professional costs)
- Losses on sale of fixed assets
- Remuneration unpaid within nine months after the end of the accounting period
- Expenditure not wholly and necessarily in course of the trade
- Expenditure deducted in accounts which is a general precautionary provision which has yet to materialise or is in respect of capital losses
- Interest and pension payments unpaid at year end

The following would be deducted from the profits in the accounts:

- Capital allowances
- Profits on sale of fixed assets
- Dividend income received from other UK companies
- Interest and pension payments paid in year which were unpaid at end of prior year.

## Capital Expenditure

It is difficult to decide when expenditure is of a capital nature. Just because expenditure is deducted in the accounts of the business and has not been included as an asset in the balance sheet does not mean that expenditure can be treated as allowable in the calculation of taxable profits. There is a great deal of difference between what the business man would regard as capital in accordance with accepted best accounting practice and what tax law regards as capital.

In general, tax law will seek to treat as capital any expenditure that could be regarded as the creation, modification or improvement of a fixed asset. Such expenditure may be disallowed in the computation of profits but may then as capital be eligible for capital allowances. The Inland Revenue would thus commonly review the repair and replacement expenditure of a business with a view to disallowing any capital expenditure contained therein. The gulf between accounting conventions and tax law is particularly wide on property where only limited capital allowances are permitted. The law treats most structural alterations to property as capital even where property is dismantled and many minor changes may strictly be capital in tax law even if there is no increase in the value of the asset itself.

Another type of expenditure which tax law would regard as capital would be expenditure incurred in buying and selling the trade or a part thereof as well as costs of restructuring the capital of the business or the ownership of the business. Furthermore, tax law regards abortive expenditure of these types as capital.

## Income tax of Trades, Professions and Vocations for Partnerships and Sole Traders

### *Trades, Professions and Vocations for Partnerships and Sole Traders (Schedule D, Cases I and II)*

The basis of taxing business has been simplified so that new businesses starting after 5 April 1994 are taxed on their actual profits. For such businesses, and for all other businesses from 6 April 1997, the amount assessed will be the amount of profit of the accounting year ending within the fiscal year of assessment.

For existing businesses at 5 April 1994 the new rules will not come into effect fully until 1997/98 and such businesses will be able to take advantage of the old rules that enable them to minimise their tax liabilities under the complex rules set out below.

There are also complex transitional arrangements governing existing businesses over the period running up to 1997/98, covering the assessment of 1996/97 and the accounting year ending within 1995/96. Detailed anti-avoidance provisions are in place to prevent exploitation of the transitional rules.

With these changes superimposed upon complex existing rules and transitional arrangements, it is necessary to take proper professional advice in order to minimise tax liabilities.

The old rules which still apply to businesses that started prior to 6 April 1994 are as follows:

## Year in which business starts

The amount assessed is the amount of profit during the period from start-up to the following 5 April.

## First complete fiscal year for which business carried on

The amount assessed is the amount of profit for the first twelve months of business.

## Subsequent years

1. If:
    - there is a 12-month account prepared to a date in the previous fiscal year and
    - this account started when business started or immediately after the accounts which were taken as the base of assessment for the previous fiscal year and
    - there is no other account ending in the previous fiscal year

    the amount assessed is the profit from those accounts.

2. If the three conditions above are not all present, the Inland Revenue may select any period of 12 months ending in the previous fiscal year and the amount assessed will be the amount of profit for that period.

## Fiscal years after business commences: taxpayer's option

The taxpayer may request that the assessments for the second and third years of assessment are based on the amount of profit for the actual fiscal years. The request must be for both the years and can be made at any time up to six years after the end of the third year.

## Fiscal year in which business ceases

The amount assessed is the amount of profit from 6 April preceding cessation until the date of cessation. However, where the cessation is on or after 6 April 1997 then the new rules will apply.

## Fiscal years before business ceases: Inland Revenue option

For the two years preceding the year in which the business ceases, where that cessation is on or before 5 April 1988, the Inland Revenue may, if the aggregate profit for those two fiscal years exceeds the aggregate profits assessed, revise both years so that assessments are on the actual profit for the fiscal years. Where the business ceases in the 1989/99 fiscal year the option to revise to actual is limited to 1996/97 only. After 5 April 1999 the new rules apply in full and the Inland Revenue option ceases.

## Partnerships

Where there is a change in the membership of a partnership, either by one or more partners leaving or by one or more new partners joining, the business is treated as having ceased and a new business begun. However, if at least one person is a member of the partnership before and after the change, and if all the partners before and after the change so elect, the business will be treated as continuing throughout. An election must be made within two years of the change. If an election is made it can be withdrawn within the same period. Farmers see page 71.

If after 19 March 1985:

- there is a change in a partnership
- at least one person is a partner before and after the change
- the law applies so as to treat the business as a new business from the date of change

the above rules are modified. The profit assessable for the tax year in which the new business is deemed to commence and for the next three years will be the amount actually earned in each of these years. For later years the procedure in 'subsequent years' above will apply. The 'taxpayer's option' above will apply for years five and six.

For new partnerships commencing on or after 6 April 1994, or from 6 April 1997 for all other businesses, a change in the membership of the partnership no longer causes a cessation for tax purposes and an election for continuation is no longer necessary.

## Business Losses

There are several ways in which relief may be claimed in respect of losses incurred by an individual or a partnership carrying on a trade, profession or vocation. It is advisable to have experienced professional assistance when considering which method of claim is likely to be most beneficial.

For a loss to qualify for relief the business must be operated on a commercial basis with a view to profit. For the 'new business' relief there must also be a reasonable expectation of profit. In a business of farming or market gardening, relief may be refused in some cases if losses are made for more than five consecutive years.

In general, capital allowances may be taken into account in such a way as to increase the amount of loss or convert a profit into a loss. However, if the trade consists of leasing or includes leasing, capital allowances on the leased assets may not be set against income, other than income from plant leasing, unless the trade is carried on for at least six months and the claimant devotes a substantial part of his time to it.

If a partnership makes a loss each partner may, subject to certain conditions, decide which method of claim for relief he wishes to make for his share of the loss. There are rules to restrict the tax losses of a limited partner (ie one who is not entitled to take part in the management of a trade, and who therefore has limited liabilities) to the actual financial loss suffered by the partner.

A broad summary of the options available is as follows:

1. **Same year set-off:** When a loss arises after 5 April 1990 which is allowable against general income for 1990/91 or a year later, it can be set only against the income of the person incurring the loss. It cannot be set against the income of that person's husband or wife. For years 1991/92 and later, a claim may be made to set any unrelieved losses against capital gains arising in the same year. A claim for this relief must be made within two years.

2. **Following year set-off:** For a business which started before 6 April 1994, if the person still carried on the business in the year following the year of loss, the loss may be deducted, in a similar manner to 'same year set-off', from the income and gains of that later year. If a person claims this relief, it is given in priority to 'same year set-off' for the year of claim. This relief is not available for 1996/97 and later years.
Relief must be claimed within two years of the later year (ie the year of claim).

3. **Prior year set-off:** For a business which started on or after 6 April 1994, the loss may be deducted in a similar manner to 'same year set-off' from the income and gains of the preceding year. However, any loss arising in that preceding year would take priority. For businesses which started before 6 April 1994, this relief is available for 1996/97 and later years and must be claimed within 22 months (ie by 31 January) of the year of loss.
Relief must be claimed within two years of the year of loss.

4. **Carry forward:** If losses have not been utilised in other ways, a claim may be made to carry them forward and reduce the profit of later years from the same business. Losses carried forward must be utilised as soon as possible even if they reduce income which, by virtue of personal allowances, would have suffered no tax.
Claims must be made within six years.

5. **Transfer of a business:** If the trade in which losses have been incurred is transferred to a company in exchange for the issue of shares in the company, the losses may be carried forward and set against income which the individual subsequently receives from

the company. Losses can only be set against income for a year throughout which the relevant shares are owned and they will be set against earned income in priority to unearned income.
Claims must be made within six years from the date of cessation of the trade.

6. **Terminal losses:** When a person finishes in business, losses incurred in the final twelve months may be carried back and deducted from income from the business for the three previous years. The losses are deducted from the latest year first. Claims must be made within six years from the date of cessation of the trade.

7. **Agricultural lettings:** If deductible expenses exceed assessable rent etc, the excess may be set against other income for the same or the next year. Alternatively, it can be carried forward against future income from farming or ownership of agricultural land.
Claims for set-off must be made within two years.

## *Partnership Assessments*

A single assessment under Case I or II of Schedule D is made on a partnership which started on or before 5 April 1994 and which has not suffered a tax cessation since that date. For the purposes of deciding what allowances shall be given and what tax rates apply, the amount of the assessment is shared among the partners.

The assessment will not normally be on the amount of profit for the tax year (in most cases it will be on the amount of profit earned in the accounting year ending in the previous tax year), but the apportionment is made by reference to the way in which profits are shared among the partners during the tax year.

For 1996/97 special transitional rules apply to businesses which started before 6 April 1994. The partnership assessment will usually be based on the average of the amount of profit earned during the two accounting periods ending during the tax year (ie the average of the current and previous years' profits).

With the advent of self-assessment (see page 19) from 1997/98 assessments will be made on individual partners, based on their respective shares of profit earned in the accounting year ending during the tax year, as disclosed on the partnership tax return.

Partnership assessments will also no longer apply, from 1994/95, to partnerships commencing on or after 6 April 1994.

## Sub-contractors in the Construction Industry

In order to try to minimise tax evasion in the construction industry the law requires certain people to operate a scheme of deducting tax when making certain payments and paying that tax to the Inland Revenue. The people required to operate this scheme are those whose trading activities include 'construction operations' but, in addition, some businesses which are customers for construction work can be required to operate the scheme if they spend an average of over £250,000 a year on the construction, extension etc of premises for their own use. 'Construction work' also includes demolition, site clearance and so on.

Anybody operating the scheme must ask those who do 'construction work' for them to produce an exemption certificate (known as a 714) and in many cases to give an approved voucher (form 715) when receiving payment. If the sub-contractor does not produce the certificate, the operator should withhold tax from the payment for labour (but not from payment for materials or VAT), pay the net earnings to the sub-contractor, and pay the tax deducted to the Inland Revenue. The sub-contractor will be given credit for the tax deducted when his own tax returns and accounts are submitted and liability is agreed.

Tax should be deducted at the basic rate but care should be taken early in the year if the basic rate is not the same as the year before. At the start of the year the rate is the previous year's basic rate and the date at which the change is made is later than the change-over date for PAYE.

Anybody carrying out, or intending to carry out, relevant work may apply to his tax inspector for a 714. From August 1998 a system of mandatory registration cards will be introduced for subcontractors who do not hold an exemption certificate, thus ensuring that appropriate tax is deducted at source. The inspector will need to be satisfied that the person can be relied upon to keep proper business records and to meet his fiscal responsibilities and will take into account the person's tax history. A company which satisfies the inspector will get either a certificate 714C or 714P. A member of a partnership will get a 714P. An individual may get either a 714I or a 714S. If the certificate is a 714S, the amount which may be paid without deduction of tax is limited to £150. Tax should be deducted from any balance.

Vouchers 715 should be obtained from all certificate holders except holders of 714C. The vouchers should be sent weekly to the Inland Revenue Liverpool Computer Centre. Where tax is deducted, it should be accounted for monthly in the same way as PAYE and operators must therefore register for PAYE even if they have no employees.

## Farming and Agricultural Profit

### *Farming Profits*

Farming profits are notoriously volatile and income tax, charged on the sliding scale, can be inequitable to farmers. Therefore, in an attempt to even out the peaks and troughs, a system of averaging profits was introduced. If the taxable profits for two successive tax years differ by more than 30 per cent of the higher figure, then the farmer can choose to have the tax for each year based on half the total profit. This treatment must apply to both years.

If the figure for the lower year exceeds 70 per cent of the higher year but does not exceed 75 per cent, the difference between them is multiplied by three. Three-quarters of the higher figure is deducted, and the resultant figure is subtracted from the higher year and added to the lower.

This treatment only applies to profits from farming and market gardening, not to profits derived from other business activities on the land. The profits to be averaged (and to be looked at to see whether there is the essential 30 per cent difference between each year) are the profits before adjustment is made for losses (eg brought forward), capital allowances or balancing charges. There is a time limit for claiming the relief: two years from the end of the second of the two tax years concerned.

It is not possible to skip a year. The years to be averaged must be two successive years. If there is a loss, this is treated as a nil result. This is in fact a helpful provision because it ensures the benefit of averaging but at the same time leaves the loss available for set-off against other income.

'Averaging' claims cannot be made for a year of commencement or cessation. The later of the two years in an averaging claim may become the earlier of two years in a subsequent claim, when it is the adjusted figure which enters into the second calculation.

## *Herd Basis*

Livestock kept by farmers is normally treated as part of their trading stock in calculating profits subject to income tax. Thus, the cost of buying animals will be a deduction in calculating trading profits, while the proceeds of sale of animals are brought in as receipts. The 'herd basis' option enables production herds to be treated in effect as capital assets. This is favourable to the farmer who realises a profit on the disposal of his herd which, as a capital profit, will be free of income tax. It will also be free of capital gains tax on the footing that the animals disposed of are chattels (or tangible moveable property). Conversely, the effects may be unfavourable for the farmer who has to dispose of his herd at a loss because this will be taken into account neither for income tax nor for capital gains tax.

Particular points to note are:

1. The special treatment applies to 'production' animals and birds, ie those kept for the produce of the living animal (wool, milk, eggs, etc) or for its young.
2. There is a time limit of two years for applying related to the time when the herd is first taken into account for income tax purposes.

The election relates to one particular herd and, once made, cannot be revoked (but see point 3 below).

3. Briefly, the mechanics of the reliefs are that the cost of the herd itself and the cost of additions are not taken into account for tax purposes, but the cost of replacements is deductible from taxable profits. The proceeds of sale of the whole, or a substantial part, of the herd are not generally taken into account for tax purposes, but subject to this the proceeds of sale of an animal will be treated as a trading receipt. If the herd is kept going, the proceeds of sale of animals disposed of should normally be more than balanced by the deductible cost of replacements. There are, however, elaborate rules for dealing with the gradual run-down of a herd; immature animals; those bred by the farmer; the treatment of different types of herd; cases where a herd is disposed of and a new one acquired; compulsory slaughter; and the inevitable anti-avoidance provisions covering transfers to companies, family partnerships etc.

An election for the herd basis should only be made after the long-term tax implications have been considered carefully.

## Commercial Woodlands

In broad terms, the commercial use of woodlands is now outside the tax system. Investment in this type of enterprise should theoretically be based purely on commercial and environmental grounds rather than fiscal grounds. However, given the right circumstances, it might still be attractive to have a form of income which is tax free.

## Capital Allowances

The cost of providing or improving fixed assets is not, on normal accountancy principles, an expense which can be deducted in calculating the profit of a business, but depreciation of assets is deducted. For tax purposes, the depreciation is taken out of the profit and loss account, thus increasing the profit, but for many assets the taxpayer can claim capital allowances instead. Capital allowances are generally claimed on a reducing balance basis of 25 per cent per annum. For instance, an asset worth £4,000 would attract £1,000 capital allowances in the first year, then £750 (£4,000 – £1,000 x 25 per cent) in the second, and so on. Where rates of depreciation are less than 25 per cent, in the earlier years for which an asset is used in business, the taxable profit is likely to be less than the commercial profit. In later years this will be reversed.

It is not compulsory to claim the full allowances which are available and it is advisable to obtain experienced professional advice to see when claims should be foregone, in order to improve the position for a later year. One class of asset on which capital allowances are available is described as 'plant and machinery' but this covers a much wider range of assets than might be assumed, such as many types of fixtures, fittings, equipment, apparatus and vehicles. In some circumstances it can even cover alterations to a building because of installation of plant. From 30 November 1993, rules were introduced to clarify the boundary between plant on the one hand and buildings on the other. The former of which are eligible for capital allowance at 25 per cent (a far higher rate than buildings which either may not be eligible at all or are only subject to a writing down allowance of 4 per cent). There are also circumstances where a lessee of a building incurs cost on installing plant (which becomes a landlord's fixture) and can claim capital allowances.

## Balancing charges

Balancing charges are negative capital allowances. They are charges made when the sale proceeds (or, sometimes, the open market value) of assets disposed of exceed unallowed costs (ie the original cost of the asset, less capital allowances already granted). Balancing charges will not exceed capital allowances previously given.

A balancing charge will not be made on the disposal of an industrial building, a hotel or a commercial building in an enterprise zone if the disposal takes place more than 25 years after the building was first used. For a building on which the construction expenditure was incurred before 6 November 1962 the period is 50 years.

Table 14 shows the allowances applicable for recent years on industrial buildings, and Table 15 those on plant and machinery.

The writing down allowance given on agricultural buildings and works which can be offset against trading income is 4 per cent per annum.

Patent rights acquired before 1 April 1986 attract a writing down allowance which can be offset against trading income and amounts to the full cost written off in equal instalments over 17 years or the remaining life of the rights, if less. After 31 March 1986, the allowance is 25 per cent of written down value each year. The balancing allowance, if rights come to an end, is the residue of cost. If rights are sold, the residue of cost less sale proceeds.

The writing down allowance given on furnished lettings, which can be offset against trading income, is 10 per cent of rents less water rates or any other tenants' burden borne by the landlord. This a non-statutory allowance permitted by the Inland Revenue.

## Table 14 Industrial building allowances

| If the claimant is the person who incurred the costs of construction | Expenditure incurred (or contract entered into) within 10 years of the site being included in an enterprise zone | Initial allowance | 100% |
|---|---|---|---|
| | | Writing down allowance | 25% of cost |
| | Other industrial buildings and constructions | Writing down allowance | 4% of cost (2% if cost was before 6 November 1962) |
| If the claimant is a person who has subsequently acquired the interest of the person who incurred the costs | | Writing down allowance | Residue of cost* divided by number of years from date of purchase to 25th (or 50th) anniversary of first use |
| All claimants | | Balancing allowance less sale proceeds | Residue of cost* less sales proceeds restricted to cost |
| Hotels | | Same as industrial buildings | |
| Commercial buildings in enterprise zones | | Same as industrial buildings in enterprise zones | |

*A balancing charge is added to (or a balancing allowance is deducted from) the vendor's residue before sale in order to give the purchaser's residue after sale.

## Table 15 Plant and machinery allowances

| Items used for entertaining | | Nil |
|---|---|---|
| Other items | First year allowance<br>Writing down allowance | 25%<br>25% of reducing balance |
| Motor cars | Writing down allowance | 25% of reducing balance but maximum of £3,000 for cars bought after 10 March 1992 (£2,000 maximum if prior) |

The writing down allowance given on scientific research, which can be offset against trading income, is 100 per cent. This covers all capital expenditure, including building and plant but excluding land and dwelling houses, for trading activities in the field of natural or applied science for the extension of knowledge.

The writing down allowance given on know-how, which can be offset against trading income, is 25 per cent of the reducing balance, as for ordinary capital allowances.

## Private Cars

Due to a relaxation of rules on allowances to an employee using his own car for business purposes, employees are entitled to relief for running costs of a private car under normal Schedule E expense rules, in addition to capital allowances.

### Business Economic Notes

A Tax Inspector has an obligation to satisfy himself that business accounts are correct. This can sometimes be very difficult. In order to assist him the Board of Inland Revenue prepares 'Business Economic Notes'. These give him some idea of the way in which various businesses often operate, including legal matters specific to particular trades, and conventional practices.

When examining business accounts the Inspector will pay regard to these notes, and any business where the results or any particular features of the accounts appear not to conform with what is expected, is likely to be the subject of a detailed enquiry. It is therefore desirable that traders and/or their accountants are familiar with such notes and that they examine accounts critically in the light of such notes before sending them to the Inland Revenue. It is also possible that such examination might highlight weaknesses in the operation of the business. Alternatively, if any particular business does not conform to the norm, it is advisable to consider the reasons for this and to explain these reasons to the Inspector when sending in the accounts. This should help to reduce the chance of that business being selected by the Inspector for a detailed investigation.

# 4

# National Insurance

Overview — Class 1 — Class 3 — Classes 2 and 4 — the Self-employed — Maximum contributions — Company cars and Class 1A

## Overview

National Insurance (NI) is a further tax on earnings. It is an important tax that raises substantial amounts of revenue for the government. In September 1995 the government announced further measures as part of its move to deregulation and simplification of the tax system. There will be more co-operation between the two departments (IR and DSS) and future Budget tax changes will not attract NIC and IR dispensations and some statutory concessions will apply to NIC.

The range of benefits in kind (see pages 57-9) and other payments to employees that are subject to National Insurance will be gradually extended and this trend is expected to continue. The Chancellor has closed the loophole whereby certain payments of benefits in kind were made by 'gold bullion' and other devices intended to avoid the payment of National Insurance. Certain loopholes are believed to still exist.

There are currently four classes of contributions. Employees and their employers pay Class 1 contributions through the PAYE system. There is a scale of tax for the employee of up to 10 per cent on earnings up to £455 per week. There is no upper limit on the employer's contributions, which are on a scale of up to 10.2 per cent of earnings. It is intended that the rate of employers national insurance will decrease slightly in 1997 from 10.2 per cent to 10 per cent. There is a reduced scale for both employee and employer when employees are members of an approved company pension scheme, and this is known as the 'contracted-out rate'.

Under Class 2 contributions, a flat rate of £6.05 per week is payable by the self-employed, who can choose to pay by direct debit or be billed quarterly.

Class 3 is a flat contribution rate of £5.95 per week paid voluntarily by those who seek to maintain or increase their future entitlement to certain State benefits.

Class 4 is another form of National Insurance contributions paid by the self-employed which is calculated at 6 per cent on their taxable profits above £6,860 up to a limit of £23,660.

## Class 1

Contributions for employed persons are paid by both the employee and the employer. The employer deducts the contribution along with PAYE tax. No contributions are due in respect of people earning below a 'lower earnings limit' which for 1996/97 is £61 per week. There is also an 'upper earnings limit' of £455 per week. For the portion of earnings above this figure, employer's contributions must be made, but not employee's contributions. For children under 16 neither employer's nor employee's contributions are payable. For men over 65 and women over 60 employer's contributions are payable, but not employee's contributions.

Table 16 *The weekly rates of NI Class I contributions (1996/97)*

| Weekly earnings | Employee's contribution ||| Employer's contribution ||
|---|---|---|---|---|---|
| | First £61 % | Balance if not contracted out % | Balance if contracted out % | Not contracted out % | Contracted out rate % |
| £61 to £109.99 | 2 | 10 | 8.2 | 3.0 | 0 |
| £110 to £154.99 | 2 | 10 | 8.2 | 5.0 | 2.0 |
| £155 to £209.99 | 2 | 10 | 8.2 | 7.0 | 4.0 |
| £210 to £455 | 2 | 10 | 8.2 | 10.2 | 7.2 |
| Over £455 | No additional liability ||| 10.2 | * |

* £34.59 plus 10.2% on excess above £455

## Class 3

Certain people who are not required to pay other classes of contribution at any given time are allowed to pay voluntary contributions in order to maintain or achieve entitlement to certain State benefits (for example, a higher level of state retirement pension for individuals who have spent some time abroad). The 1996/97 rate of voluntary contributions is £5.95 per week.

## Classes 2 and 4 – the Self-employed

A self-employed person is required to pay a flat rate weekly contribution (Class 2) and also a contribution based on taxable income (Class 4). The latter is assessed by the Inland Revenue along with the income tax assessment under Schedule D Case I or II (see previous chapter). The taxable income for Class 4 contributions is that after adjusting for capital allowances and balancing charges.

The 1996/97 rates for men under 65 and women under 60 are as follows:

| | |
|---|---|
| *Class 2* Flat rate | £6.05 per week. Nil when profits are below £3,430 in the year. |
| *Class 4* Profit-related | 6.0 per cent of profit between £6,860 and £23,660. Maximum is therefore £1,008.00 (6.0 per cent of £23,660 minus £6,860). |

## Maximum Contributions

If a person has more than one source of employment or has employment as well as self-employment the maximum amount of contribution by him (excluding employer's contribution) is £2,152.86. The maximum Class 4 (self-employed, profit related) contribution is limited to a figure which, when added to Class 1 (employee) and Class 2 (self-employed, flat rate) contributions, totals £1,328.65. If Class 1 and Class 2 already exceed this amount, Class 4 is nil.

## Company Cars – Class 1A

An employer has to pay national insurance on company cars and fuel provided to employees. The payment for 1996/97 is due on 19 June 1997. The basis of this charge is 10.2 per cent of the car scale charges under income tax Schedule E (see page 60).

The fuel scale charge is payable when the individual is provided with fuel for private use and is charged as set out in the table on next page.

*80/Tax Facts*

Table 17 *Fuel scale charges (£) (1996/97)*

| 1996/97 | Petrol | Diesel |
|---|---|---|
| **1,400cc or less** | 72.42 | 65.28 |
| **1,401cc to 2,000cc** | 90.78 | 65.28 |
| **Over 2,000cc** | 134.64 | 83.64 |

# 5

# Corporation Tax

*Overview — Rates — Close companies — Purchase of own shares by an unquoted trading company*

## Overview

Corporation tax is payable by companies on their profits at rates of 33 per cent, or for small companies at 24 per cent. Profits are computed in a similar manner to those for income tax, with deduction of most trading expenses being allowed.

Corporation tax started in 1965 and the present system in 1972. It is payable nine months after the company year-end except for an advance payment when the company pays a dividend or distribution to its shareholders. This advance corporation tax (ACT) reduces the tax payable nine months after the company year-end.

Corporation tax is assessed on the chargeable profit of companies resident in the UK and also on certain profits of some non-resident companies if they carry on a trade in the UK. For UK companies, 'chargeable profit' means the whole of the income (except any dividends receivable from another UK company) and also capital gains. The tax year runs from 1 April to 31 March and the rates are shown in Table 18 (page 83). From 1 October 1993 'Self Assessment' was introduced (see 'Pay and File' page 83). Any capital gain is liable to tax and realised losses on chargeable assets are deducted from gains. If losses exceed gains they are carried forward and deducted from gains in later years.

If a company makes a trading loss (which is calculated after the deduction of capital allowances), it may deduct the amount of the loss from any other profits (including capital gains) which it may have for the same accounting period. Alternatively, it may carry the loss forward and deduct it from subsequent profits of the trade in which the loss was incurred. If that does not wholly use the loss, the balance of the loss can be carried back to the profits of the company for the three previous years or can be surrendered to another company in the same group to be relieved against its profits of the same period.

If an investment company has subscribed for shares in an unconnected qualifying trading company and it incurs a loss on those shares which is allowable for capital gains tax it will, in certain circumstances, be able to set the loss against income of the relevant period and the preceding year.

Some of the income (eg some types of interest) which a company receives may have suffered deduction of income tax at source. Such income is included in the corporation tax assessment but credit is allowed for the income tax deducted.

Small companies pay a lower rate of tax of 24 per cent. In deciding whether a company is small its total profits are taken into account. Total profits means the profit assessable for corporation tax plus any dividends received from other UK companies (other than companies within the same group). A company with profits too big to qualify as a small company (£300,000) may be entitled to some 'tapering relief'. The relief is 9/400th of the amount by which the total profit falls short of £1,500,000. The fraction is multiplied by the profits chargeable to corporation tax and divided by the total profit. Where there are associated companies for tax purposes the figures of £300,000 and £1,500,000 are divided by the total number of companies concerned.

See page 84 for the treatment of close investment-holding companies.

## Rates

Table 18 shows the corporation tax rates for the last three years and the rate for small companies. Tapering relief is available on the rate for companies above the small company threshold but below a further limit.

### *Advance Corporation Tax (ACT)*

When a company pays a dividend it must pay tax known as advance corporation tax (ACT) to the Inland Revenue. ACT is based on the lower income tax rate which operates from 6 April to 5 April. Although the corporation tax rules apply for a financial year from 1 April to 31 March, from 6 April 1994 the ACT rate is ¹/₄ of the dividend, which equates to the lower rate of income tax (20 per cent) and the tax credit attached to the dividend.

Table 18 *Corporation tax rates for the 3 years ending 31 March 1997*

| Year to 31 March | Standard rate % | Small company rate on profits % | Max profit to qualify for small company rate £ | Max profit to qualify for tapering relief £ | Fraction of tapering relief | Fraction of ACT for year to 5 April |
|---|---|---|---|---|---|---|
| 1995 | 33 | 25 | 300,000 | 1,500,000 | 1/50 | 1/4 |
| 1996 | 33 | 25 | 300,000 | 1,500,000 | 1/50 | 1/4 |
| 1997 | 33 | 24 | 300,000 | 1,500,000 | 9/400 | 1/4 |

For the collection of ACT, the year is divided into four or five parts. These are the periods ending 31 March, 30 June, 30 September, 31 December and the accounting date of the company if it is not one of these dates. When a dividend is paid during one of these periods the ACT must be paid within 14 days after the end of the period.

Since companies can choose their accounting date, their profits are calculated for the accounting period ended on that date. Accounting periods cannot exceed 12 months so, if a company makes up its accounts for a longer period, that period is split into two accounting periods – the first of 12 months and the second of the remaining months to the accounting date.

The profits are taxed, as seen previously, for financial years and the profit of any accounting period is time-apportioned between the financial years covering the accounting period.

ACT paid by a company on dividends paid during its accounting period is regarded as a payment on account of the tax for the period and is deducted from the tax ultimately due. The amount to be deducted is restricted to the equivalent of the lower rate of income tax on the company's profits. Thus if a company has an accounting period ending 5 April 1996 and is assessed on total profits of, say, £30,000, the maximum ACT which can be deducted from the tax charged is £6,000. Where the accounting period bridges a date on which the rate of ACT changes the profits are time-apportioned and the maximum ACT calculated at the rate applicable for each period.

ACT which cannot be set off is carried forward and credited against tax due in later years. Alternatively, it can be carried back to the six previous years. In some cases, the benefit of surplus ACT can be surrendered to other companies in a group. In some groups of companies, elections can be made which allow dividends to be paid within the group without the payment of ACT.

## *Pay and File*

Pay and File applies for companies with accounting periods ending on or after 1 October 1993. Interest is charged on any corporation tax paid later than nine months after that company's year-end. This necessitates the payment of an estimate of a company's corporation tax liability by the normal due date (ie nine months after the end of the accounting period), even where no assessment has been raised, and the submission of accounts, tax returns and computations within twelve months of the end of the period of account.

Pay and File introduces severe fixed and tax-related penalties for non-compliance where no return is received. Failure to notify chargeability within 12 months of the end of the period of account carries a penalty not exceeding 100 per cent of the unpaid tax. Where returns have been received but are submitted late there are fixed penalties. These are between £100 and £500 from 12 months after the end of the accounting period in addition to fixed penalties of between £200 and £1,000. There are tax-related penalties of 10 per cent of unpaid tax from between 18 to 24 months which increases to 20 per cent of unpaid tax where the return is submitted more than 24 months after the end of the accounting period. These may be reduced by losses of the next year being carried back against profits of the year in question.

## Close Companies

A close company is, broadly, a company which is director-controlled or which is controlled by five or fewer people. For this purpose certain relatives and associated persons are treated as the same person. Control usually refers to over 50 per cent of the voting power but there are also other meanings.

A company which is a 'close investment-holding company' (CIC) is taxed wholly at the standard rate of 33 per cent on profits.

### *Loans to Participators (usually a shareholder or loan creditor)*

If a close company makes a loan to a participator it will be required to pay the Inland Revenue an amount which corresponds to the prevailing ACT fraction. The payment will be due nine months after the year end. When the participator repays the loan (or part of it), repayment of the tax can be reclaimed from the Inland Revenue. This treatment extends to indirect loans, including the settling of debts of the participator or advancing money to a third party who in turn does something to benefit the participator. If the participator is also an employee or director it is possible that he may also be charged to tax on a 'beneficial loan' (see page 58).

## Purchase of Own Shares by an Unquoted Trading Company

The 1981 Companies Act permits a company to purchase its own shares. Normally, for tax purposes, if a company repays to a shareholder more than the amount subscribed for a share, the excess is treated as a distribution. As the Government wanted to make the process easier it introduced a tax relief which is conditional upon certain criteria being established. A brief summary of the principal criteria is as follows:

- The company must be a trading company or the holding company of a trading group. The trade must not consist of dealing in shares, securities, land or futures.
- The vendor must be resident and ordinarily resident (see pages 51-2) in the UK.
- The vendor must have owned the shares for at least five years. If he acquired them under the will or intestacy of a deceased person, the period of ownership by the deceased is taken into account.
- If the vendor does not part with all his shares, his interest as a shareholder must be substantially reduced. Broadly, this means that his fractional share of the capital after the sale should not be more than 75 per cent of his fractional share before the sale.
- After the sale the vendor must not control more than 30 per cent of the capital or the voting power in the company.
- The transaction must be made primarily for the benefit of the trade of the company and must not be part of a scheme of tax avoidance.

If all these conditions are met, the sale will not be treated as giving rise to income. The sale will come within the capital gains regulations (see next chapter).

It is possible, and advisable, to apply for clearance in advance when wishing to take advantage of this legislation.

# 6

# Capital Gains Tax

Overview — Self Assessment — Indexation — Rates — Payment — Chargeable assets and exemptions

## Overview

Capital gains tax, which was introduced in 1965, is a tax payable on the profit arising on the disposal of a chargeable asset after deducting the costs of disposal. The broad intention of the legislation is to relieve from tax any gain attributable to the period of ownership of an asset up to 31 March 1982 and tax the subsequent gain after allowing for indexation to compensate for increases in the retail price index from that date.

It is the intention of the Chancellor to abolish capital gains tax and, at least as far as the proprietors of private company businesses or for those who invest in such businesses, he has gone a long way towards that goal in the last few years.

The gain or loss on the disposal of each asset is calculated separately.

Everything acquired prior to 1 April 1982 is now normally based on the market value at 31 March 1982, which must be estimated or negotiated where necessary.

It may happen that, as a result of the introduction of rebasing at 31 March 1982, a larger gain is calculated on a disposal than would have been calculated if the law had not been changed or that a larger loss is calculated than would have been calculated on the old basis. In such cases the old provisions, based on original cost, market value at 6 April 1965 or time apportionment of a gain from that date still apply. If the new provisions produce a loss where otherwise there would have been a gain or produce a gain where otherwise there would have been a loss, the law operates to treat the transaction as giving rise to neither a gain nor a loss.

If a person does not want the provisions of the previous paragraph to apply he can elect that all assets which he owned at 31 March 1982 are treated as acquired by him on that date at their then market value. Such an election is irrevocable. It must be made within two years from the end of the fiscal year in which the first disposal of a chargeable asset (other than certain exempt disposals such as that of a main residence) is made. The Board of Inland Revenue has the power to accept even later elections.

## Self Assessment

Self Assessment starts on 5 April 1996 for the year 1996/97. Under these arrangements tax returns and the calculation of taxes due and payments for both income tax and capital gains tax will be combined. This is outlined in Chapter 1 (pages 19-22).

## Indexation

The theory of capital gains tax is that a gain or loss is calculated by comparing acquisition value (ie normally, cost price plus expenses of acquisition) plus any later enhancement expenditure with disposal value (ie normally, sale price less expenses of disposal). In certain cases, market value at the acquisition date (or, if later, at 31 March 1982) or disposal date is taken instead of cost price or sale price.

A further deduction is a figure calculated by adjusting the acquisition value and enhancement expenditure for the movement in the retail price index. This movement is measured from the month of acquisition or enhancement until the month of disposal, in percentage terms. This is done by dividing the index at sale by the index at acquisition or enhancement, as set out in the table below.

Table 19 *The retail price index 1984–95*

|  | 1984 | 1985 | 1986 | 1987 | 1988 | 1989 | 1990 | 1991 | 1992 | 1993 | 1994 | 1995 |
|---|---|---|---|---|---|---|---|---|---|---|---|---|
| January | 86.8 | 91.2 | 96.2 | 100.0 | 103.3 | 111.0 | 119.5 | 130.2 | 135.6 | 137.9 | 141.3 | 146.0 |
| February | 87.2 | 91.9 | 96.6 | 100.4 | 103.7 | 111.8 | 120.2 | 130.9 | 136.3 | 138.8 | 142.1 | 146.9 |
| March | 87.5 | 92.8 | 96.7 | 100.6 | 104.1 | 112.3 | 121.4 | 131.4 | 136.7 | 139.3 | 142.5 | 147.5 |
| April | 88.6 | 94.8 | 97.7 | 101.8 | 105.8 | 114.3 | 125.1 | 133.1 | 138.8 | 140.6 | 144.2 | 149.0 |
| May | 88.9 | 95.2 | 97.8 | 101.9 | 106.2 | 115.0 | 126.2 | 133.5 | 139.3 | 141.1 | 144.7 | 149.6 |
| June | 89.2 | 95.4 | 97.8 | 101.9 | 106.6 | 115.4 | 126.7 | 134.1 | 139.3 | 141.0 | 144.7 | 149.8 |
| July | 89.1 | 95.2 | 97.5 | 101.8 | 106.7 | 115.5 | 126.8 | 133.8 | 138.8 | 140.7 | 144.0 | 149.1 |
| August | 89.9 | 95.5 | 97.8 | 102.1 | 107.9 | 115.8 | 128.1 | 134.1 | 138.9 | 141.3 | 144.7 | 149.9 |
| September | 90.1 | 95.4 | 98.3 | 102.4 | 108.4 | 116.6 | 129.3 | 134.6 | 139.4 | 141.9 | 145.0 | 150.6 |
| October | 90.7 | 95.6 | 98.4 | 102.9 | 109.5 | 117.5 | 130.3 | 135.1 | 139.9 | 141.8 | 145.2 | 149.8 |
| November | 90.9 | 95.9 | 99.3 | 103.4 | 110.0 | 118.5 | 130.0 | 135.6 | 139.7 | 141.6 | 145.3 | 149.8 |
| December | 90.9 | 96.0 | 99.6 | 103.3 | 110.3 | 118.8 | 129.9 | 135.7 | 139.2 | 141.9 | 146.0 | 150.7 |

Note: Retail price index for March 1982 was 79.44.

## 88/Tax Facts

The application of the indexation allowance has served to reduce a gain or increase a loss, or sometimes to convert a gain into a loss. However, as from 30 November 1993, an underlying gain can only be extinguished by indexation. It cannot be converted into a capital gains tax loss nor can indexation be used to increase a capital loss which is now limited to the underlying capital gains tax loss before indexation.

### Rates

The aggregate of the chargeable capital gains less the allowable capital losses of an individual for a fiscal year are subject to the deduction of an annual exemption and the assessable gains are taxable as the top slice of income (except that no personal allowance or deductions relating to income tax can be set against it), ie 20 per cent, 24 per cent or 40 per cent or a mixture of these rates. Companies pay at the appropriate rate (see page 83).

Settlements are taxed at 24 per cent unless they are discretionary or accumulation trusts (see page 33) in which case they are taxed at 34 per cent. Settlements do not benefit from the new 20 per cent income tax rate band and they normally have half of the annual exemption available to an individual (see below). However, when the settlor or his spouse retain an interest in the settlement then capital gains are taxed on the settlor at the rate applicable to the settlor.

### Payment

Capital gains tax is due for payment by an individual or trust on 1 December following the tax year ending on 5 April in which the capital gain occurs. For payments by companies, see previous chapter. From 1996/97, as a part of the simplification of the tax system, payment dates for capital gains tax and income tax will become identical. For interest on overdue tax see page 47.

### Chargeable Assets and Exemptions

Chargeable assets are all forms of property including options, debts, currency (other than sterling) and property created without being acquired (eg goodwill) but excluding certain items. The main exemptions are:

- Principal private residence with land up to half a hectare (1.235 acres) or a larger area in some cases. See page 91.
- A dwelling which since before 6 April 1988 has been the sole residence of a dependent relative and is provided for that relative rent free and without any other consideration.
- Winnings from betting, lotteries, premium bonds, etc.

- Ordinary private motor vehicles.
- National savings certificates, yearly plan and children's bonus bonds.
- Gilt-edged securities, qualifying corporate bonds and options relating thereto.
- Life assurance policies and deferred annuity contracts disposed of by the original beneficial owners.
- Compensation or damages for a wrong or injury.
- Grants for giving up agricultural land under a statutory scheme.
- Tangible moveable property with a disposal value not exceeding £6,000. If the value exceeds £6,000 the gain is limited to five-thirds of the excess.
- Tangible moveable property with a predictable life of 50 years or less (but this exemption does not cover commodities on a terminal market or business assets on which capital allowances have been claimed).
- Assets given to charities, museums, universities, etc.
- Business Expansion Scheme (BES) shares.
- Enterprise Investment Scheme (EIS) shares on first sale.
- Quoted shares in a Venture Capital Trust (VCT).
- Personal Equity Plan (PEP) investments.
- Tax Exempt Special Savings Accounts (TESSAs).
- Debts (other than 'a debt on a security') in the hands of the original creditor. A 'debt on a security' has a complex definition but broadly it means that it is for a fixed term and amount and the terms are such that the debt is capable of being marketed, sold or assigned at a profit or loss.
- Foreign currency which was acquired for personal use.
- Decorations for valour and gallant conduct (unless the person disposing had bought the decoration).
- Shares in certain (mainly close) companies which are transferred to approved 'employee trusts'.
- Trees on woodlands occupied on a commercial basis.

## *Annual Exemption*

For 1995/96 the first £6,000 of net chargeable gains is exempt from tax. For 1996/97 the exemption is increased to £6,300. Husband and wife are each entitled to a separate exemption.

Losses brought forward are deducted only to the extent necessary to reduce the resultant net gains to the amount of the annual exemption.

An exemption of £6,300 is available to the personal representatives for the gains on the estate of the deceased in the remainder of the tax year following the death of the deceased and the two following tax years.

A settlement for the benefit of a disabled person is normally treated in the same way as an individual.

Any other settlement which was made before 7 June 1978 is entitled to an exemption equal to half that of an individual (ie £3,150 for 1996/97). For settlements made after 6 June 1978 the amount of the exemption will depend upon how many other settlements the settlor has made. The allowance (half the individual's allowance) is divided between the settlements, subject to the minimum allowance for each, being one-tenth of an individual's figure.

## Losses

Losses incurred in a fiscal year are set against gains of the same year to calculate the net gains or losses for the year. If there is an overall net loss it is carried forward to set against gains of later years. However, it will not be set against a gain which, because of the exemptions referred to above, would not suffer tax. Thus, for instance, if there were a loss of £4,000 brought forward from 1995/96 and the aggregate gains in 1996/97 were £6,600 only £300 of the loss would be used to set against the gain reducing it to £6,300 which would be covered by the annual exemption. The balance of the loss of £3,700 would be carried forward to set against 1997/98 and/or later years.

If an individual has subscribed for unquoted shares in a qualifying trading company and he subsequently makes a loss on their disposal, he may apply to treat that loss as reducing his income for the year of disposal or the following year. It is treated as reducing earned income in priority to investment income.

The loss must be incurred in a 'disposal at arm's length' for full consideration, or in winding up, or upon the value of the shares becoming negligible.

Claims must be made within two years of the year of disposal.

If a loss arises in the year of death it can be carried back and set against gains of the previous three years (latest year first). As with losses carried forward, the loss carried back will not be used to set against gains to the extent that no tax is chargeable on the gain by virtue of the annual exemption.

## Death

Assets passing on death are deemed to be acquired by the legatees or trustees at probate value but no capital gains tax is chargeable on the estate of the deceased by virtue of any consequent uplift in value.

## Husband and Wife

If assets are transferred from one spouse to the other, the spouse making the transfer is deemed to have sold the asset at a price which gives no profit or loss and the other spouse is deemed to have bought it at a price which gives no profit or loss.

Each spouse is taxed separately and is entitled to his/her own exemption. Losses of one cannot be set against gains of the other.

## *Principal Private Residence*

No gain is taxable on the disposal by an individual of a dwelling with gardens or grounds of up to half a hectare (1.235 acres) which throughout his period of ownership has been his principal private residence and which has not been used for other purposes. This exemption does not, however, apply if the home was bought wholly or partly for the purpose of realising a gain by selling it. If money is spent on the property wholly or partly for the purpose of enhancing its sale value, that part of the gain attributable to the money spent is not exempt.

If a person has more than one home and it therefore becomes necessary to determine which is his principal residence he can determine the matter by giving notice to his tax inspector within two years of the date from which he had more than one home. He can subsequently vary the notice but only for a period starting not less than two years before the date of the notice. If the individual does not give notice, the inspector can decide which is the principal residence and for what periods. He must notify such decision in writing and the individual has 30 days in which to appeal, if he so chooses, to the General or Special Commissioners. (The General Commissioners are an independent body of local business people appointed by the Lord Chancellor as mediators where appeals against assessments cannot be agreed between the appellant and the inspector. The Special Commissioners normally meet in London and have a greater knowledge of the law).

Land of more than half a hectare may qualify for exemption if the Commissioners are satisfied, having regard to the size and character of the property, that the further land was necessary for its reasonable enjoyment as a residence.

If part of the land of under half a hectare is sold, the gain will normally be exempt. If part of the land which comprised more than half a hectare is sold, the sale will only qualify for exemption if it can be shown that at the time of its acquisition it was necessary for its reasonable enjoyment as a residence. If the house is sold but part of the land is retained and sold later, the later sale will not be exempt whether or not the original holding was of less than half a hectare.

If there is a lodger who is treated as a member of the family (eg has meals with the family and has use of living rooms) the fact that he pays for accommodation is ignored for capital gains tax (though not for income tax, but see Furnished Lettings and the Rent-a-Room relief, page 41) and will not prevent the exemption from applying. If part of a house is let to someone who is not treated as a member of the family, the part of a gain attributable to the let part of the home (determined by area, rather than value) is exempt up to a maximum of £40,000 (or up to the gain attributable to the unlet part if that is less than £40,000).

If some part of the property is used exclusively for other purposes (eg as business premises) the part of the gain attributable to that part is not exempt. Exemption is not lost if a part of the property is used both for domestic and for business purposes.

If a property has not been used as a private residence for periods during the ownership, the gain may have to be apportioned between qualifying and non-qualifying periods. However, there are generous rules to treat some absences as part of a qualifying period even though the property may have been let. These include:

- the period of absence of up to 12 months following acquisition due to alterations or decoration or delay in selling the previous home;
- the whole of the last 36 months of ownership;
- absences before 31 March 1982 if the sale is after 5 April 1988;
- periods of absence of up to three years provided that there is qualifying occupation both before and after the absence periods and that during those periods there was no other home on which exemption could be claimed;
- absences in certain situations because of employment or business requirements.

## *Replacement of Business Assets (Rollover Relief 1)*

If the proceeds of certain business assets are used to acquire other business assets the gain can, subject to certain conditions, be deducted from the cost of the new assets so that tax is not paid at the time. In such a case, if the new asset is subsequently sold, the gain on the old asset as well as the later asset will be assessed.

The relevant types of asset are:

- land and buildings
- fixed plant or machinery
- goodwill
- milk and potato quotas
- ewe and suckler cow quotas (sold after 1 January 1993)
- ships
- aircraft
- hovercraft
- satellites, space stations and spacecraft (including launch vehicles).

The assets must be used for a business (including commercial forestry). If there is a part of the asset which was not so used or if the asset had for some period been used for a non-qualifying purpose, the gain is apportioned to see what part of it can be 'rolled over'.

## Incorporation of Business (Rollover Relief 2)

If an individual transfers to a company a business as a going concern together with all the assets (or all the assets except cash) in exchange for shares in the company, any gain on the disposal of the assets is calculated but not assessed. The cost of the shares for future capital gains tax purposes would normally be the value of the consideration (ie the business assets, including goodwill) given for the shares, but it is reduced to take account of the gain calculated on the transferred assets. In effect, therefore, the gain on the disposal of original assets is deferred until there is a disposal of the substituted assets (the company shares).

## Re-investment Relief (Rollover Relief 3)

The relief applies where there is a capital gain and the proceeds are invested in shares in an unquoted company. It is possible to hold over the payment of capital gains tax until the shares in the company are sold. This relief was introduced in the March 1993 Budget in a restrictive form. However, the rules were relaxed substantially in the November 1993 Budget. The Chancellor in 1994 removed further restrictions that bring the relief more into line with the Enterprise Investment Scheme.

With effect from 29 November 1993 the re-investment relief from capital gains tax applies where a taxpayer makes a capital gain on the disposal of assets of any description. He is able to defer any chargeable gain where this is re-invested in shares in a qualifying unquoted trading company or qualifying share quoted on AIM (Alternative Investment Market). There are no restrictions on the number of shares in the qualifying unquoted or AIM trading company that he needs to acquire. The re-investment in shares may take place within a year prior to, or three years after, the disposal of the asset giving rise to the capital gain. For every £1 invested, the capital gain is reduced by £1 with the actual tax saving being dependent upon the rate at which capital gains tax is paid by the taxpayer. The main types of non-qualifying companies are subsidiaries and financial concerns so capital gains cannot be deferred where the proceeds are invested in these type of companies.

The main effect of this relief is that capital gains tax can be deferred until the shares in the qualifying unquoted or AIM trading company are subsequently sold. This treatment should be contrasted with the more generous treatment of the Enterprise Investment Scheme and Venture Capital Trusts which not only allow the roll over of capital gains but also grant a further tax relief of 20 per cent on the initial investment and exemption from capital gains on the subsequent sale of the shares (see page 41). The aim of re-investment relief, the Enterprise Investment Scheme and Venture Capital Trusts is to promote the development of a business culture that encourages the start-up and expansion of small companies.

## Part Disposals of Land

Complicated rules apply where only part of a piece of land is disposed of. Generally the remaining part of the land has to be valued for the purpose of allocating the cost to the parts disposed of and retained.

In the case of land, where the amount or value of the consideration does not exceed one-fifth of the total value, the person making the disposal can claim that no assessment is made but what would have been the 'disposal value' is deducted from the 'cost' of the whole – thus leaving the possibility of a larger tax liability on any future disposal. This claim cannot be made if the sale proceeds (or value) are over £20,000, if it is an inter-spouse or inter-group transfer or in the case of a lease with less than fifty years to run.

Again in the case of land, the Revenue will accept an alternative method of calculating the gain on a part disposal. The parts disposed of and retained may be treated as separate assets where there is a fair and reasonable means of apportioning the original cost (or 31 March 1982 value) between the two parcels of land.

## Compulsory Purchase of Land

If land (other than that which is tax-exempt as part of a principal private residence) is disposed of to an authority exercising or having compulsory powers and the vendor uses all or part of the proceeds to acquire other land the gain can, subject to certain conditions, be deducted from the cost of the replacement land. Tax on the gain is in effect deferred until there is a disposal of the replacement land.

## Holdover Relief

Holdover relief is available on gifts of the following types of asset or donee:

- Gifts to any donee of business assets. This category includes assets used for a business carried on by the donor or his family company. It also includes shares in his family company or in an unlisted company. It does not include transfers to non-residents or to companies which are controlled by non-residents.
- Gifts of any assets which are not potentially exempt transfers for inheritance tax (see page 98). This category will include transfers to discretionary settlements.
- Gifts of any assets to political parties and to certain public bodies or for public benefit.

Where a person makes a gift (which term includes a sale for less than full value) and the holdover relief is not available he may have to pay tax and, as he received no money (or little money), this may cause hardship. There are provisions for paying the tax in instalments in some cases. Tax that remains unpaid by the donor within 12 months of the due date may be collected from the donee within two years of the original due date. The donee then has a right to recover the tax paid by him from the donor.

## Registered Housing Associations

If a person transfers land to a non-charitable housing association for less than its full market value the difference is not brought into charge to capital gains tax. The gain is calculated by reference to the actual proceeds received from the housing association, even though this may be below market value.

## Non-residence

Tax on capital gains is not chargeable on a person who is not resident (and, in the case of an individual, not ordinarily resident) in the UK (see pages 51-2) even if the assets disposed of are located here – except to the extent that the asset in the UK has been used for the purposes of a trade carried on through a branch or agency in the UK and that trade has been carried on during the fiscal year in which the disposal took place.

Tax is chargeable on such assets if the trade ceases, or if they are removed from the UK. Tax is also chargeable in respect of UK assets used for a profession or vocation.

Beneficiaries of non-resident settlements can be treated as having received capital gains in certain circumstances if they receive capital from the settlements.

## Retirement

Retirement relief is available if a person who has attained the age of 50 (55 prior to 28 November 1995), or who has to retire earlier on the grounds of ill-health, disposes of certain business assets at a gain.

If the person has held the assets and satisfied certain conditions for ten years, the first £250,000 of the gain is exempt. So also is half of the next £750,000. For a period of less than ten years (but at least one year) a fraction of the ten-year relief is available.

Shares in a personal company are included as assets which can qualify for relief. Assets which have been used as business assets by a personal company or partnership can similarly qualify. So can assets which a person owned and used for the purposes of an employment. Shares in a personal company qualify only if the individual has been a full-time working officer or employee of the company (or, if the company is a member of a group or commercial association of companies). This means that he must have been required to devote most of his time to the service of the company or companies in a managerial or technical capacity. If a person who has been a full-time working officer or employee takes semi-retirement but continues to work for at least ten hours per week he may still claim relief if he satisfies the other qualifying conditions. A personal company is one in which the individual can exercise at least 5 per cent of the voting rights.

Husband and wife are entitled to relief independently. Therefore, in the most extreme case the combined reliefs may be as much as £2,000,000. If an individual's entire interest in a business or his/her entire shareholding has passed to the other spouse, the qualifying period of ownership can be calculated by adding the successive periods of each spouse. If, however, the passing is other than on death, entitlement to exemption will not start until the younger of the two spouses is 50.

# 7

# Inheritance Tax

Overview — Transfer of value — Returns — Rates — Payment — Spouses — Lifetime gifts — Gifts with reservation — Exemptions — Business property relief — Wills and intestacy — Insurance — Trusts — Overseas aspects

### Overview

Inheritance tax is a tax on certain 'transfers of value' made during a person's lifetime and on the value of the estate passing on death. 'Transfers of value' include:

- gifts;
- sales or other dispositions made at less than market value;
- failure to exercise rights; and
- indirect ways in which a person allows his wealth to be diminished and that of somebody else to be increased.

A reduction in wealth will not be treated as a transfer of value if it can be demonstrated that it was not intended to confer a gratuitous benefit on another person. Some acts which might otherwise be regarded as transfers of value are specifically excluded within defined circumstances. They include:

- waivers of remuneration;
- waivers of dividends; and
- grants of tenancies of agricultural property.

The rate of tax on lifetime gifts is 20 per cent and that on death is 40 per cent. If the donor pays the tax on a lifetime gift, that is treated as a further gift so that tax is charged at an effective rate of 25 per cent of the value of the gift itself. On both the 'lifetime' and the 'death' scales tax is only chargeable once a threshold is reached. This is £154,000 for 1995/96 and increased substantially to £200,000 for 1996/97. The threshold relates to the cumulative total of gifts or transfers at the time concerned and during the seven years ending on that date.

Recent years have seen a substantial change in the treatment of shares that are unquoted or on AIM. With effect from 6 April 1996 such shares, whether voting or non-voting, or whether the holding is small or large, will effectively be outside the scope of inheritance tax. Such shares will be given a 100 per cent business property relief which on death will write down their value for inheritance tax to zero. The main prerequisites will be that the shares must be held for two years and the company must be a trading company. It is difficult to see how this treatment can continue indefinitely in the future.

Gifts to individuals and certain settlements (see page 33), eg children's accumulation and maintenance trusts and trusts for the disabled, are known as 'potentially exempt transfers' and are free of tax when made. They are, however, charged to tax retrospectively if death occurs within seven years of the gift being made.

If an individual makes a gift of an asset in such a way that there is a 'reservation of benefit', the asset is, subject to certain exceptions which would otherwise be exempt transfers, still brought into charge on death, however long the period between the gift and the date of death.

## Transfer of Value

When a transfer of value does occur during the lifetime of an individual, it is put into one of three categories:

1. **Exempt transfers.** See list on page 104.
2. **Potentially Exempt Transfers (PETs).** These are transfers from one individual to another (other than exempt transfers between spouses, see page 104) or from an individual to an interest-in-possession trust, an accumulation and maintenance trust or a trust for a disabled person. No tax is payable in respect of a potentially exempt transfer unless the donor dies within seven years of the date of the transfer. If that happens, the value of the transfer is added to the estate passing on death.
3. **Chargeable transfers.** These are all other transfers (eg cash or other assets given to a discretionary trust).

### Gifts with reservation

Special rules apply where:
- possession and enjoyment of the property given is not bona fide assumed by the donee immediately; or
- where the property given is not enjoyed by the donee to the entire exclusion (or virtually to the entire exclusion) of the donor; or
- the donor continues to benefit from the property.

Until such time as the reservation is removed, such property is still regarded as that of the donor. On removal he is treated as making a PET. The exception to the above rule is where the gift would otherwise be an exempt transfer (see page 104) by reason of any exemption other than the annual exemption or the normal expenditure out of income exemption. In such a case gift with reservation rules do not apply.
The reservation would not prevent tax from being paid on the original gift, if appropriate, eg a chargeable transfer.

Gifts with reservation are explained in greater detail on page 103.

## Returns

No inheritance tax return is required in respect of an exempt lifetime gift or a potentially exempt transfer. Returns of chargeable lifetime gifts exceeding £10,000 in the year (or £40,000 in the last ten years) are due within twelve months of the end of the month in which the gift was made. On death a return must be submitted by the personal representatives, within twelve months of death. Subject to certain conditions no return is required if the estate is valued at £145,000 or less. In addition, when someone dies, the recipient of a gift made within the previous seven years, or of a gift with reservation, is required to submit a return.

## Rates

The rates of tax for 1996/97 on the excess value over and above the nil rate band (see below) are as follows:

| | |
|---|---|
| On death | 40 per cent on cumulative transfers over £200,000 |
| On lifetime chargeable transfers | 20 per cent on cumulative transfers over £200,000 |

If the donor pays the tax on a lifetime transfer it is at a rate of 25 per cent of the net figure in excess of the available nil rate band.

### *Nil Rate Band*

This is the amount on which no inheritance tax is payable. In recent years the nil rate band has been:

| | |
|---|---|
| 10 March 1992 to 5 April 1995 | £150,000 |
| 6 April 1995 | £154,000 |
| 6 April 1996 | £200,000 |

### *Tax on Death*

On death, the position for the previous seven years is reviewed. All potentially exempt transfers in the period are listed, together with all chargeable transfers in the period and the estate passing on death (subject to the various exemptions, business and agricultural property relief, and the exemption for assets passing to the spouse, see below). Tax is recalculated according to the rates prevailing at the time of death. The tax is abated for transfers made between three and seven years before death, but not so as to reduce the tax on any chargeable lifetime transfer to below what it was at the time of the transfer. (See 'Gifts within seven years of death' page 102.) Where freehold or leasehold property is sold for less than probate value within four years of death (one year for quoted investments) the sale price may be substituted for the value at the date of death as the inheritance tax base.

## Quick Succession Relief

Where there has been a chargeable transfer on which tax has been paid and the recipient dies within five years, there may be some relief if his (the second person's) estate is, by virtue of the earlier transfer, greater than it would otherwise have been.

The relief takes the form of reducing the tax on the death of the recipient relating to the appropriate part of his estate by a proportion of the tax suffered on that part on earlier death or transfer. The proportions are:

| | |
|---|---|
| Transfer up to one year before death | 100 per cent |
| Transfer between one and two years before death | 80 per cent |
| Transfer between two and three years before death | 60 per cent |
| Transfer between three and four years before death | 40 per cent |
| Transfer between four and five years before death | 20 per cent |

## Payment

Table 20 shows the date when payment of inheritance tax is due.

Table 20 *Inheritance tax due dates*

| | |
|---|---|
| Lifetime transfers between 6 April and 30 September | End of April in following year |
| Lifetime transfers between 1 October and 5 April | 6 months after the end of the month of transfer |
| Increase, following death, of tax paid on transfers within 7 years before death and tax on potentially exempt transfers | 6 months after the end of the month of death |
| Other tax on death | On delivery of their account by personal representatives |

## Tax Payable by Instalments

In certain cases it is possible to pay the tax by ten equal annual instalments, the first instalment being payable on the normal tax payment date. The property qualifying for payment of tax by instalments on death is as follows:

- Land and buildings
- Shares or securities in a company controlled by the deceased
- Minority interests in an unquoted company which bear at least 20 per cent of the tax, or where the tax cannot be paid without undue hardship
- Minority interests in an unquoted company with a value of more than £20,000 which represent at least 10 per cent of the share capital
- A business or a share in a business where the qualifying conditions for 100 per cent business property relief have not been met.

Apart from land and buildings not forming part of a business or qualifying for agricultural relief, no interest is due on the outstanding instalments except if instalments are paid late.

Where death occurs within seven years of a potentially exempt transfer, the instalment option is available provided the transferee still has the qualifying property at the time of the transferor's death or, if earlier, his own death.

The donor (in the case of a lifetime gift) or the personal representatives (on death) are primarily liable to the Inland Revenue for the tax, although the recipient of the assets may have to pay in the event of their default.

## Rates of Interest on Overdue Tax

When tax is paid after the date it is due, interest, for which no tax relief is available, may be charged based on the period when the tax remains due but unpaid, based on the following rates of interest:

|  |  |
|---|---|
| 6 July 1989 to 5 March 1991 | 11 per cent |
| 6 March 1991 to 5 May 1991 | 10 per cent |
| 6 May 1991 to 5 July 1991 | 9 per cent |
| 6 July 1991 to 5 November 1992 | 8 per cent |
| 6 November 1992 to 5 December 1992 | 6 per cent |
| 6 December 1992 to 5 January 1994 | 5 per cent |
| 6 January 1994 to 5 October 1994 | 4 per cent |
| 6 October 1994 onwards | 5 per cent |

## Spouses

It is important to realise that each spouse can enjoy the benefit of the nil rate band and also various lifetime exemptions. Where the couple are sufficiently wealthy, it is therefore often considered that each should have enough of the joint wealth to take maximum advantage of these reliefs. Assets can be freely transferred between spouses (unless the recipient is not domiciled in the UK) without suffering tax so it is usually quite easy to ensure that each has personal ownership of whatever level of wealth is thought appropriate. Transfers between spouses must be genuine changes in ownership so, if the donor has any reservations about the durability of a marriage, this must be borne in mind.

It is possible, within two years of a death, for a 'Deed of Variation' to be made which, in effect, enables the will to be rewritten. A Deed of Variation cannot, however, be used to reduce the entitlement under the will of any children under the age of 18 years without an application to the Court.

## Lifetime Gifts

### Gifts more than seven years before death

Under inheritance tax, certain gifts are free of tax if made more than seven years before death. They are:

- Gifts to individuals
- Gifts to qualifying accumulation and maintenance settlements
- Gifts to trusts in which an individual has a right to income as it arises
- Gifts to certain trusts for the disabled.

Other gifts (eg those to discretionary settlements) are charged to tax when made, at half the rate applying on death, but are disregarded in calculating the rate of tax on death if made more than seven years before death.

### Gifts within seven years of death

If death occurs within seven years of a gift, then the value of the gift when made is charged to tax at the rate applicable on death. If, in the case of a chargeable transfer, this tax calculation produces a higher liability than that levied on the occasion of the gift, then the excess is payable. If, on the other hand, it produces a lower liability, there is no refund of tax already paid.

It may be that the value of the property given away has reduced between the date of the gift and the date of death. In such cases, it is possible to make a claim to have the tax calculation at the date of death based on that reduced value – if it were not so it would be possible for the tax liability levied on the owner of the asset to exceed its value.

To accompany the 'writing off' of gifts after seven years, there is a 'tapering relief' whereby gifts made between three and seven years before death are charged to tax at a lower rate. The relief takes the form of a reduction in the tax chargeable on the gift, rather than in the value on which tax is charged. Table 21 shows the relief.

Table 21 *The tapering relief for gifts made 3–7 years before death*

| Years between gift and death | Tapering relief % |
|---|---|
| More than 3, less than 4 | 20 |
| More than 4, less than 5 | 40 |
| More than 5, less than 6 | 60 |
| More than 6, less than 7 | 80 |

It is only where the original gift is so large that it exceeds the available nil rate band that any benefit is received. The availability of this relief does not reduce the tax payable on the assets actually passing on death as the cumulative total of gifts taken into account in computing the value on which tax is chargeable is not affected.

## Gifts with Reservation

The reservation of benefit rules are designed to prevent the making of gifts with strings attached. For example, parents cannot make a gift of the family home to the children, the parents continuing to live there rent-free. The reservation of benefit rules apply if an individual makes a gift and either:

- possession and enjoyment of the property is not assumed by the donee at least seven years before death; or
- at any time in the seven years before death the property is not enjoyed by the donee virtually to the entire exclusion of the donor.

If it is shown that there has been a reservation of benefit in respect of a gift, the asset will be treated as remaining in the donor's estate at the date of death (unless the reservation ceased more than seven years before death). The asset will then be included in the estate at the value at the date of death and not the value when given away. If tax was paid when the gift was originally made (eg because it was made to a discretionary trust and was therefore not a potentially exempt transfer), this is deducted from the liability payable on death.

There are instances in which the reservation of benefit rules do not apply. These are:

- If the gift is one of a class of exempt gifts, eg a gift to a spouse. Gifts within the annual exemption (ie gifts from one person not exceeding £3,000 per annum), however, are caught, as are gifts within the normal expenditure out of income exemption.
- In the case of land or chattels, continued occupation or enjoyment by the donor is ignored if he pays a market rent for the asset. Such a rent will of course be subject to income tax in the hands of the recipient.

- If it is possible to split property into different interests, one of which is gifted without reservation and the other retained. This is not possible under Scottish law. It has been suggested that in England and Wales a reversionary lease may be granted to a beneficiary which will not come into possession for a number of years (not exceeding 21) and the freehold (which will gradually decrease in value) may be retained by the donor.

The reservation of a benefit to the spouse of a donor does not appear to make the benefit liable to tax either. However, a Government spokesman did say in the course of the parliamentary debates on the Finance Bill in 1986 that if the donor shares the spouse's benefit, then the rules would apply.

## Exemptions – Exempt Transfers

### Seven-year write-off

Lifetime gifts to individuals and non-discretionary trusts are exempt from tax when made and are disregarded in determining the tax payable on death provided that the donor survives for seven years. Chargeable lifetime transfers (eg to discretionary trusts) are similarly disregarded after seven years. As husband and wife are treated separately for inheritance tax purposes, they can each make chargeable gifts equal to the nil rate band (£154,000 until 5 April 1996, £200,000 thereafter) every seven years without any tax liability.

### Spouse

Unless the recipient is domiciled (see page 51) outside the UK and the donor is not, there is no tax levied on gifts between spouses, whether made during lifetime or on death. This exemption can be very useful in cases where one of the spouses has insufficient assets to make gifts. Care must, however, be taken not to make the gift to the spouse conditional upon the asset being passed on to the children, as otherwise the Inland Revenue may seek to tax the gift.

### Annual exemptions

Every individual has an annual exemption of £3,000 which can be set against lifetime gifts. If it is not used in any year it may be carried forward to the following year but no further. The maximum deduction for annual exemptions is accordingly £6,000. If a potentially exempt transfer becomes chargeable because death occurs within seven years, then the value of the gift taxed by reason of the death will be reduced by any available annual exemptions for the year of the gift and the previous year.

## Small gifts

Small gifts to an individual of no more than £250 are exempt, provided that the total of gifts (per donor) to that individual does not exceed £250 in the tax year.

## Normal expenditure

There is an exemption for gifts made as part of normal expenditure provided that they are made out of income and leave the transferor with sufficient income to maintain his usual standard of living. This exemption can be particularly useful to cover the payment of premiums on life policies written in trust, of deeds of covenant, and so on. Although payments must be made on a regular basis, they need not be made to the same donee.

## Other exemptions and reliefs

- Gifts to charities and qualifying political parties
- Certain waivers of dividends and remuneration
- Quick succession relief (see page 100)
- Loans repayable on demand
- Dispositions for the maintenance of the family
- Certain gifts for national and public purposes, and of qualifying heritage property
- Certain gifts in consideration of marriage:
  — by parent of bride or groom         £5,000
  — by grandparent of bride or groom    £2,500
  — by any other donor                  £1,000
- Certain gifts to housing associations.

## Business Property Relief

This is a most important area of tax planning in the private business. This relief covers all shares in an unquoted qualifying company and the relief extends to cover companies on the Unlisted Securities Market and the Alternative Investment Market. From 6 April 1996 relief is given at the rate of 100 per cent, regardless of the size of holding.

'Business property' may include an interest in an unincorporated business (ie sole trader, profession or partnership) or shares and securities in a quoted or unquoted company. A business not carried on for gain is specifically excluded. Land, buildings, machinery or plant which, immediately before the transfer, were used wholly or mainly for the purposes of a business carried on by a partnership in which the transferor was then a partner or by a company controlled by him also qualify for relief, but at the lower level of 50 per cent.

Tax charged on transfers of business property can often be paid by ten annual instalments free of interest. Rates of business property relief will vary according to circumstances, as shown in Table 22.

The relief is not available for investment companies, or companies or businesses carrying on a trade of land or share dealing. The property in question must normally have been owned for a minimum of two years before it qualifies for relief. However, if the property was acquired on the death of the spouse, the period of ownership of the deceased spouse is aggregated with that of the transferor. The fact that this relief is now given at 100 per cent in most cases means that the owners of such shares must give great thought to how they would wish to deal with their shares in the future. Relief at this rate is equivalent to an exemption in the death situation. However, 100 per cent relief may not survive in the longer term, so careful thought needs to be given to the situation over the next year and before the next election.

Table 22  *Business property relief*

| Transfers of, or out of | Relief after 6 April 96 % | Relief after 9 March 92 % |
|---|---|---|
| Sole trader's or partner's interest in an unincorporated business | 100 | 100 |
| Controlling interest in a fully quoted company | 50 | 50 |
| Holdings exceeding 25% in qualifying unquoted, USM and AIM companies | 100 | 100 |
| Minority holdings of 25% or less in qualifying unquoted, USM and AIM companies | 100 | 50 |
| Land, buildings, machinery or plant used by a firm in which the transferor is a partner or by a company controlled by him | 50 | 50 |

The inheritance tax rules contain an important business property relief provision which can trap the unwary. This arises when a lifetime gift is made which qualifies for business property relief (or would have qualified if not a potentially exempt transfer). If death subsequently occurs within seven years, inheritance tax on the gift will be calculated by reference to the death rates (subject to tapering relief if the transferor has survived for at least three years). However, when the tax is calculated on death, business property relief will not be available unless the property has been retained by the donee and continues to qualify for relief up to the date of death. Relief is retained if the property has been disposed of but replaced within three years by other qualifying assets which are held at the donor's death.

Property will not qualify for business property relief if it is subject to a binding contract for sale. Agreements between shareholders, for example to buy out the shares of a deceased member, should be avoided, although it may be possible to use options to achieve a similar result without loss of relief.

## *Business Transfers and their Value*

For inheritance tax purposes the value of a transfer is based on the reduction in the estate of the donor, which is not necessarily the same thing as the value of the gift to the recipient. Perhaps the most marked demonstration of this difference (ignoring any 100 per cent business property relief that may be available) is in the case of close company shares. If a person who owns 57 per cent of the ordinary share capital of a typical company gives away 5 per cent, his estate will have been reduced by the difference between the value of 57 per cent and the value of 52 per cent. If he then gives away another 5 per cent, the reduction in the second case is the difference between the value of 52 per cent and the value of 47 per cent. This second transfer is likely to be much bigger than the first because he has lost control of the company and all his remaining shares have been effectively devalued. Each recipient will have 5 per cent of the shares and the value of this holding in their hands will normally be quite a lot less than the reduction in the donor's estate on each occasion.

## *Related property*

A further principle of valuation which is often of importance is that of 'related property', which requires that, in deciding the basis of valuation, shares held by the spouse must be taken into account. Thus, for example, if husband and wife each own 40 per cent of the shares in an unquoted company, the value of each shareholding will be computed as one half of an 80 per cent holding, which will normally give a substantially higher figure than valuing a 40 per cent holding. This example is also subject to any 100 per cent business property relief that may be available.

## *Lloyd's Underwriters*

A Lloyd's underwriter has to deposit assets with Lloyd's as security for his underwriting activities, and will also have assets in the form of reserve funds and undrawn profits. As he is regarded for inheritance tax purposes as carrying on a business, his estate is normally entitled to the 100 per cent business property relief on the value of his qualifying

Lloyd's assets, and may include the collateral backing any guarantee or letter of credit. However, relief will be restricted as regards 'excessive' assets and often has to be individually negotiated. If Lloyd's assets are left by will to the surviving spouse, the benefit of this relief on a subsequent transfer or death will be lost once the assets are paid to her (or him), and so the drafting of the will in these cases can be very important.

## Woodlands

Woodlands which are managed on a commercial basis and exempt from income tax are eligible for 100 per cent business property relief in the same way as any other business interest. A special relief for woodlands held on death which defers the tax until a subsequent sale or death is rarely advantageous, particularly where business property relief is available.

## Farming

Successive Governments have long recognised the particular difficulties which farmers face in funding death duties by providing special reliefs for agricultural property. The level of the relief was extended in 1992.

There is a detailed definition of agricultural property qualifying for relief, which includes:

- agricultural land or pasture;
- ancillary woodland and buildings; together with
- cottages, farm buildings and farmhouses if of a character appropriate to the property.

The relief is given only in respect of the agricultural value of land and therefore excludes any possible additional value of plant, stock and so on. Such items may, however, be eligible for business property relief (see above).

### Rate of relief

If the transferor has the right to vacant possession, or the right to obtain vacant possession within twelve months, relief is available at 100 per cent of the agricultural value of the property. In other cases (eg let land) the relief is limited to 50 per cent. With effect from 1 September 1995 100 per cent relief is given to farmland subject to agricultural tenancies created on or after that date or aquired as the result of the death of the previous tenant. In addition, the property must either have been occupied by the transferor for the purpose of agriculture for the two years prior to the transfer, or it must have been owned by him for the previous seven years and occupied by someone else for agriculture during that time.

There are also special rules dealing with replacement and inherited property and relief for shares in farming companies. A further important point to watch is the risk of losing the relief if at the date of the transfer there is a binding contract for sale. Unexpected problems can arise in this area by reason of partnership agreements which, for example, provide for the continuing partners to purchase the share of a departing partner, and care is needed to avoid loss of relief.

The legislation includes a trap for the unwary. If a lifetime gift qualifying for agricultural property relief is made within seven years of death, the tax will be recomputed on death. However, the benefit of the agricultural property relief will be lost unless the property has been retained by the donee throughout and continues to qualify for relief up to the date of death. Relief is retained if the property has been disposed of and replaced within three years by other qualifying assets, which are held on the donor's death.

## Payment of tax

Tax charged on transfers of agricultural property can normally be paid by ten annual instalments free of interest.

# Wills and Intestacy

## Wills

Failure to make a will, that is, dying intestate, will result in assets passing according to the intestacy rules. These may well not coincide with the wishes of any of the individuals concerned, and may result in the payment of unnecessary inheritance tax. Even if the intestacy rules are acceptable, the administration of the estate will be greatly eased if a will has been made appointing executors. Once a will has been made it should be kept in a safe place and reviewed regularly to ensure that it is still appropriate to the individual's personal and financial circumstances and to the prevailing tax regime.

## Nil rate band

As husband and wife each have the benefit of a nil rate band, it is sensible from a tax point of view to ensure as far as possible that assets equal to at least the nil rate band are passed to the children on the first death. Extreme care should be taken in the drafting of the wording of a nil rate band legacy to ensure that it does not unintentionally include an unlimited legacy of property qualifying for the 100 per cent business property relief. In cases where the surviving spouse may require access to the funds, it may be possible for assets equal to the nil rate band to pass into a discretionary trust which can be used to benefit the survivor without forming part of his or her estate.

## Rewriting the will

It frequently happens that a will turns out to be not entirely to the wishes of the beneficiaries. It may, for example, leave the whole estate to the surviving spouse who would prefer both for financial and tax saving reasons to see some or all of the assets passing to the children. Provided that all beneficiaries are of full age and agree, it is possible to rearrange the assets within two years of death and have the revised dispositions treated as if effected by the will for inheritance tax purposes (provided that an election is submitted to the Inland Revenue within six months of the rearrangement). Such a technique can be particularly useful as a means of passing assets from the surviving spouse to children to use up an otherwise wasted nil rate band of the deceased.

## Discretionary wills

In some cases individuals know exactly how they want their estates to be distributed and they can give precise instructions for the drafting of the will. Others may prefer to give their executors (who may include the surviving spouse) absolute discretion as to the distribution of assets. Provided that the distribution to beneficiaries or appointment on other trusts is effected within two years of death, inheritance tax will be applied as though the assets had passed in this way under the will. No appointments should be made within three months of death.

## Intestacy

Table 23 gives the rules which apply in the case of intestacy (someone dying without having made a will).

In all cases where a deceased individual, who would have been entitled to benefit from an intestacy if he or she had been alive, leaves children or other issue, those children take the share of their parents at age 18 or on marriage under that age, and income up to that date.

The rules in Northern Ireland are very similar, but quite separate and substantially different rules apply in Scotland as laid down by the Succession in Scotland Act 1960, as amended.

Table 23 *Intestacy rules – England and Wales*

| Surviving relatives | Distribution |
|---|---|
| Spouse and issue | £125,000 plus personal effects to spouse. Balance: 50 per cent on trust for spouse for life and then to children; remaining 50 per cent income for children; and capital to them when they reach age 18 or marry under that age. If the children are already married or over 18 they take the assets absolutely. |
| Spouse with no issue | £200,000 plus personal effects to spouse. Balance: 50 per cent to spouse; 50 per cent to parents or (if dead) to brothers and sisters or (if dead) nephews and nieces. If none of these are living all the assets pass to the spouse. |
| Issue but no spouse | Assets are divided between the children when they reach age 18 or marry under that age. Income up to the age of 18 or earlier marriage is held on statutory trusts for the children. If the children are already married or over 18 they take the assets absolutely. |
| No spouse or issue | Assets pass to relatives in following order:<br>1. Parents<br>2. Brothers and sisters<br>3. Nieces and nephews<br>4. Grandparents<br>5. Uncles and aunts |
| No living relatives | Assets pass to Crown. |

*112/Tax Facts*

Table 24 *Intestacy rules in Scotland*

| | |
|---|---|
| **Prior rights** | |
| Surviving spouse | Rights to matrimonial home up to value of £65,000. If value exceeds £65,000, a cash sum of £65,000. |
| | Furniture and contents up to value of £12,000. If more than one house, spouse has choice of which house, furniture and contents to take. |
| | The sum of £21,000 if there are surviving children or remoter issue; £35,000 cash if no children or remoter issue. |
| **Legal rights** | |
| Surviving spouse | Legal right to half net moveable estate after debts and prior rights if no children and to one third if there are children. |
| Children | Legal right to receive one half of net moveable estate if no surviving spouse, or one third if spouse survives. |
| **Free estate (after prior rights and legal rights)** | |
| Surviving next of kin | Children, grandchildren or great-grandchildren. |
| | Parents take one half and brothers and sisters or their descendants take the other half. If neither parent survives, then brothers or sisters or their descendants take all. If no brothers or sisters etc, parents take all. |
| | Wife or husband. |
| | Uncles and aunts or their descendants. |
| | Grandparents. |
| | Great uncles, great aunts or their descendants. |
| | Great-grandparents. |
| | The Crown. |

## Insurance

The insurance industry had in past years a high profile in the marketing of arrangements designed to mitigate the effect of capital transfer tax. Although the inheritance tax legislation in general nullified the effect of certain arrangements, insurance still has its uses.

### Term assurance

The death of a donor within seven years of making a lifetime gift may result in tax becoming payable in respect of the gift and/or a higher than expected liability on the rest of the estate. There may well be an excellent case for the use of term assurance designed to cover the potential liability. The policy would be written in trust for the intended beneficiaries and the premium payments by the donor would probably be exempt gifts under the annual or normal expenditure out of income exemptions. Term assurance may also be beneficial as a protection against inheritance tax in the event of premature death, such as that of a husband and wife with young children.

## *Funding liability*

If other action to mitigate the effect of inheritance tax is for some reason impractical, and if sufficient cash is available, the decision may be taken to fund all or part of the anticipated liability on death by paying substantial premiums into a life policy written in trust for the intended beneficiaries. The payment of each premium will reduce the value of the remaining estate, and the premiums may be free of inheritance tax under the annual or normal expenditure out of income exemptions. The growth of the invested fund will take place outside the donor's estate.

## *Back to back*

Subject to liquid funds being available, an old estate duty avoidance technique may enjoy a revival under inheritance tax. This involves the taxpayer purchasing an immediate life annuity, part of the income from which is used to fund premiums on a life policy written in trust for the intended beneficiaries. The purchase of the annuity immediately depletes the value of the estate, but there is a guaranteed income for life. On death, the life policy matures free of tax in the hands of the beneficiaries. In many cases the payment of the premiums each year will be free of inheritance tax under the annual and normal expenditure exemptions. Care is needed to ensure that the purchase of the annuity and the life assurance contract are not 'associated operations' (ie two or more operations of any kind by the same person or different persons which affect the value of property transferred). In practice, the Inland Revenue does not seek to attack this type of arrangement provided that the policy is issued on full medical evidence and would have been issued on the same terms if the annuity had not been purchased.

## *Pensions*

Under a company pension scheme it is possible to arrange substantial death in service cover which can be held outside the estate so that no inheritance tax liability arises on death. If this is paid to the surviving spouse, inheritance tax liabilities on the second death may be substantially increased. In such cases it may be preferable for a letter of wishes to be deposited with the trustees of the scheme so that the funds can be appointed to the children free of inheritance tax or to a discretionary trust from which the surviving spouse could benefit should the need arise, but which would otherwise be used for the benefit of the children.

## Trusts

An individual may be reluctant to make gifts because of an unwillingness to relinquish control. In such circumstances, it may be appropriate to make a gift to a trust or settlement of which the donor or someone in whom he has confidence is a trustee.

The inheritance tax legislation divides trusts into two broad categories:

- those under which someone (eg a life tenant) has a right to receive current income; and
- those under which the trustees have a discretion as to the application of income.

### Interest in possession trusts

Gifts into a trust under which an individual is entitled to the income arising are potentially exempt transfers; so are lifetime terminations of such interest if the trust property becomes the absolute property of another individual or becomes subject to fresh trusts for an interest in possession, for accumulation and maintenance or for the disabled. Otherwise, the termination will constitute an immediate chargeable transfer. Terminations on death give rise to an immediate charge. Certain other transactions may give rise to a charge to tax, eg the artificial devaluation of trust property.

The annual and marriage gifts exemptions of the life tenant may, subject to certain conditions, be used to cover a gift through the medium of an interest in possession trust.

### Discretionary trusts

In the case of trusts where the trustees have discretionary powers, there is a 'periodic charge' to inheritance tax on every tenth anniversary of the formation of the settlement at 30 per cent of the normal lifetime rates. The maximum charge is accordingly 6 per cent every ten years. The tax charge depends principally on the value of the trust property at the relevant date and the cumulative value of chargeable transfers made by the settlor when he created the settlement. If property ceases to be held in discretionary trusts, then a proportionate periodic charge is levied which is normally based on the length of time between the last periodic charge and the chargeable event in question. Special rules apply during the first ten years.

## Accumulation and maintenance trusts

A special type of trust for young people is exempt from the normal inheritance tax charges applied to a discretionary trust. To qualify for this special treatment, the beneficiary must be entitled to receive at least the income as of right by age 25 at the latest, and in the meantime the trustees must be required to accumulate any income not paid out for his education, maintenance or benefit. Capital, however, may be retained in the trust beyond age 25.

## Reversions

A future right under a trust is normally excluded from inheritance tax. Thus, for example, where any person has a right to the capital of the trust after the death of some other person, that reversionary right can be given away without any charge to inheritance tax.

## Resident and non-resident trusts

The Finance Act 1991 contained provisions bringing the capital gains tax treatment of non-resident trusts more into line with that of resident trusts. However, there are still advantages in using non-resident trusts as a planning vehicle in the right circumstances. Although proposals to tax beneficiaries on trust gains have been abandoned, the Government is continuing its review of the other aspects of the taxation of UK resident trusts.

# Overseas Aspects

The territorial limits of inheritance tax are set by a person's 'domicile' rather than by his 'residence' – which is the concept more often applied for income and capital gains tax purposes. The basic rules are:

- if a person is domiciled in the UK, inheritance tax extends to his worldwide assets
- if a person is domiciled outside the UK, it is only the assets situated in the UK which are within the inheritance tax net.

As for income tax, there are a number of double taxation agreements with other countries to mitigate the effect of suffering tax in two countries.

## Domicile

Everyone has a domicile (and only one), and the law therefore imposes a domicile of origin on every individual when born, normally that of the father. If the parents' domicile changes, this will automatically alter the domicile of the child.

At age 16 (in Scotland 14 for a boy and 12 for a girl), a person may acquire a domicile of choice to replace his domicile of origin. However, case law shows how difficult it can often be to shake off the domicile of origin – it must be shown that the individual has moved to another territory with the intention of residing there indefinitely.

## *Deemed domicile*

The position is further complicated by special rules which can treat a person as UK domiciled for inheritance tax purposes even though he is domiciled outside the UK under general law. This will arise if he:

- has been resident in the UK for seventeen of the last twenty tax years; or
- has been domiciled in the UK at any time in the three years prior to the chargeable transfer in question.

## *Non-UK assets*

As the UK assets of a non-UK-domiciled individual are subject to inheritance tax, steps may need to be taken to ensure that any assets held are situated outside the UK. There are a variety of ways in which this might be achieved, some of which may require action being taken before a person arrives to take up permanent residence in the UK.

## *UK gilts*

The Treasury has the power to issue gilts which are exempt from inheritance tax in the hands of persons who are neither domiciled nor 'ordinarily resident' (see page 52) in the UK. As the 'deemed domicile' rules do not apply in this context, this can be a useful device for the new tax exile.

## *Trusts*

Settled property which is situated abroad is exempt from inheritance tax if the settlor was domiciled outside the UK when the trust was formed, even if the settlor subsequently acquires a UK domicile. The benefits obtainable from these arrangements may, however, be affected by the reservation of benefit rules (see page 103), and expert professional advice should therefore be taken.

## *Non-domiciled spouse*

If one spouse is UK-domiciled and the other is not, then gifts to the non-domiciled spouse will be exempt only up to a maximum of £55,000.

# 8

# Value Added Tax (VAT)

Overview — Registration — Taxable supplies — Purchases — Imports and exports — Land and buildings — Partially exempt traders — Bad debt relief — Accounting records — Private petrol benefit — Administration

## Overview

VAT is a relatively new tax to the UK but it is of growing importance. It is a European tax, the overriding law on VAT is in the EC Directives. The UK standard rate of VAT is currently 17.5 per cent, there is also a zero rate on certain goods and services and a reduced rate (currently 8 per cent) for certain supplies of fuel and power. The VAT paid by traders on their purchases can be deducted from the VAT the trader levies on his standard rated supplies. Some goods and services are exempt from VAT. The effect of exemption is that VAT cannot generally be reclaimed on purchases attributable to the making of exempt supplies. VAT is also chargeable on goods and some services imported into the United Kingdom. (For VAT purposes the Isle of Man is treated as if it were part of the United Kingdom.)

As VAT is a tax on the supply of goods and services, it should be borne in mind that the effects of any mistakes can be much more dramatic than those in calculating a tax based on profits. Also, an innocent error – or a missed deadline – can easily lead to a penalty being imposed, often calculated as a percentage of the tax underdeclared or paid late. Recent experience has shown that unexpected liabilities often arise out of transactions in property, for example, when a trader redevelops or refurbishes his business premises, lets surplus space or surrenders his lease to the landlord. Because of the complexity of the law, and because the amounts of money at stake can be very large, it is particularly important to take proper advice before entering into any property-based transaction or project.

VAT is a self-assessed tax and it is the responsibility of the trader to determine whether he needs to be registered for VAT and, if so, to take the necessary steps to register. In certain circumstances it may be beneficial for a trader to register voluntarily, so that he may reclaim the VAT on his purchases.

The law on VAT can be found in the Value Added Tax Act 1994, other Finance Acts, various Statutory Instruments and Regulations and in the European Community Directives.

VAT is administered in the UK by HM Customs and Excise who publish booklets giving their interpretation of the law. These booklets are updated from time to time and it is important to make sure that you have the current edition, together with any Amendment Sheets. One or two of the booklets have the force of law.

The scope of VAT was extended in 1994 to cover fuel and power, although the zero rate applies to most food, water, books and newspapers, new housing, transport and children's clothes.

## Registration

Not all businesses are required (or are eligible) to register for VAT. It is necessary for any new business, and any existing but unregistered business, to determine whether it is liable to register for VAT.

It is not the business itself that must register for VAT but the person who owns it. For VAT purposes a 'person' can be defined as an individual, a partnership, a corporate body, a members' club or an unincorporated association. Husbands and wives are separate persons under VAT law. You must register for VAT if your total taxable turnover from all your business activities exceeds the registration limit in force at the time. It is not possible for one person to have more than one VAT registration even if he has several totally unconnected business activities.

A person must register for VAT where:

1. Taxable turnover in the last twelve months has exceeded the registration threshold (£47,000 from 28 November 1995); or
2. Taxable turnover in the next thirty days is expected to exceed that threshold.

There are penalties for failing to register in time, as explained on pages 136-38. It is therefore essential to keep a running tally of sales, totalled monthly, so that you can tell when the registration threshold has been reached.

A point to watch is that if a new proprietor takes over an existing business, he must register for VAT immediately if the old proprietor's turnover was above the registration threshold. Sales of capital assets previously used in the business can be disregarded when calculating taxable turnover.

## *Taxable and exempt supplies*

The registration limits relate to taxable turnover. This is the total value of business supplies excluding those which are exempt. Exempt supplies include the following:

- insurance premiums and commissions
- the supply of credit, including HP commissions
- education and training (in certain circumstances)
- most medical services
- rental income
- betting and gaming and
- certain supplies of land and property.

This list is not exhaustive and only gives the broad headings under which such supplies may be exempt from VAT. The rules governing which supplies of land, buildings and building services are taxable, and which are exempt, are particularly complicated and are covered on pages 125-26. Should you think any of your supplies may be exempt you should obtain more detailed information or seek advice.

If you make only exempt supplies you are not eligible to be registered for VAT. This will be disadvantageous in that you will not be able to recover the VAT you pay out on your purchases. It is therefore essential that you correctly identify the liability of the supplies you make.

If you make both taxable and exempt supplies you will be required to register for VAT if the value of your taxable supplies exceeds the registration threshold but you will probably not be entitled to recover all the VAT you incur on your purchases (see 'Partially Exempt Traders' page 126).

## *Planning Points*

1. If you make taxable supplies which do not exceed the registration threshold, but it is in your interest to be registered for VAT, you can apply to be registered on a voluntary basis. This may be either to reclaim the VAT paid on purchases or to disguise the fact that your business is as yet only very small.

2. If you are not yet making taxable supplies but intend to do so in the future, you can apply for an advance registration, usually known as

an 'intending trader' registration. This enables you, before trading has begun, to reclaim VAT on the costs of setting up the business. An intending trader registration is particularly useful where a substantial amount of costs are to be incurred before any supplies are made.
3. VAT can usually be reclaimed both before and after registration – do not overlook this.

## Groups of companies

Two or more corporate bodies are eligible to be registered for VAT as a single VAT group providing there is common control of the group. Control is generally defined as holding a majority of voting rights.

The major advantage to group registration is that supplies between members generally are disregarded for VAT purposes. Unnecessary VAT liabilities are often created on intercompany transactions, eg paymaster services for staff salaries. Businesses must recognise that purely 'internal' charges can give a liability to VAT registration unless they are between members of a VAT group registration.

## Application for registration

All applications to register for VAT must be made on a form VAT 1, which is obtainable from any VAT office on request. The completed VAT 1 must be in the hands of the local VAT office within thirty days of:

- the end of the month in which annual turnover passed the registration threshold; or
- the day the business was taken over from another trader whose turnover was above the registration threshold; or
- the day the trader first became aware that, within the following thirty days, his turnover would exceed the registration threshold.

If a form VAT 1 has been requested, but not received within a reasonable time, you should contact the VAT office to request another. Failure to do so may lead to a penalty for late registration. Likewise if a form VAT 1 has been submitted but you have not received notification of the issue of a VAT registration number, you should contact the VAT office. It is the trader's responsibility to ensure that he obtains registration.

## Separation of business activities

As VAT registration is determined by the turnover of the 'taxable person' it may be possible to organise separate business activities as separate 'taxable persons', for example, a series of partnerships or of limited companies, as separate 'taxable persons'. If these are individually under the VAT registration limit, they will not be obliged to register for VAT. However, Customs and Excise can issue a direction that two or more businesses are to be treated as one for VAT registration purposes. This will be done where they consider that the businesses are, in reality, part of a single business and that the reason, or one of the main reasons, for splitting the business was to avoid VAT registration.

## Taxable Supplies

As explained above, taxable supplies are all supplies other than those which are exempt. However, tax is not always payable on taxable supplies. This is because some taxable supplies are zero rated – that is to say, they are chargeable to tax at 0 per cent. The difference between zero rated and exempt supplies is that any input VAT incurred in connection with zero rated supplies can be reclaimed; generally speaking, input VAT incurred in connection with exempt supplies cannot be reclaimed. Zero rated supplies include the following:

- Food (but not catering, alcohol, soft drinks, chocolate and sweets, crisps, icecream and pet foods)
- Books and newspapers
- The sale of certain buildings and the supply of certain construction services (see page 125)
- Certain alterations to, and the reconstruction of certain residential listed buildings
- Exports of goods and some overseas services
- Certain supplies by or to charities, and aids for handicapped persons
- Transport (but not taxis)
- Young children's clothing and footwear.

This list is not exhaustive. If you think that any of your supplies are eligible for zero rating you should seek further guidance.

It is most important not to assume your supplies will be zero rated unless they are specifically covered in the legislation. Should you wrongly zero rate supplies you will be responsible for paying the VAT to Customs and Excise, whether or not you can collect it from your customers. You could also be subject to penalties and interest on the amount payable (see page 136).

If your business makes supplies which are not specified by the legislation as being exempt or zero rated, they will be subject to VAT at the standard rate.

Do not forget that your VAT registration covers all supplies made. Areas where VAT is commonly overlooked are:

- Sales of capital items – for example vans, office equipment and (in certain circumstances) buildings
- Vending machine and canteen sales

*122/Tax Facts*

- Cash sales to callers
- Staff sales
- Goods taken for own use
- Goods bought or taken from stock for gifts (where the cost is in excess of £10)
- Sales of scrap.

## *Value of Supplies*

VAT is due on the total 'consideration'. If this is not wholly in money, for example, in the case of part exchange, VAT is due on what can be loosely termed the 'open market value'. This is the amount that would be payable if the full payment was in money.

VAT is also payable on goods which are given away. Normally the value is taken as the cost price of the goods. In some circumstances where the goods are given away as inducements rather than gifts, VAT is payable on the 'open market value'.

The following gifts are excluded from these rules and no VAT is due on them:

- Business gifts with a VAT exclusive cost of up to £15 which are not part of a series of gifts – eg a bottle of wine at Christmas to a customer
- Meals given free to employees
- Goods given to a charity for resale.

In the first two items above there is no supply, therefore the value of the gift is not included in your turnover or on your VAT Return. In the third, the supply is zero rated and should be included in your turnover and on your VAT return.

VAT is payable on the difference between the original purchase price and the final selling price (unless a loss arises) in the case of certain second-hand goods, such as cars, works of art, antiques, motorcycles, caravans, boats, aircraft, firearms, and horses and ponies. To benefit from this relief certain rules must be complied with and specified records kept. Failure to comply can result in VAT being payable on an amount greater than the gross margin – and even on the full selling price.

## Purchases

The general rule is that VAT can be reclaimed on all goods and services purchased for the purposes of a business (unless that business makes exempt supplies – see page 119). However, the legislation lists a number of items on which the VAT cannot be reclaimed. These include:

- The outright purchase of cars (including estate cars), other than those bought for resale as new cars or which are to be used

exclusively for business purposes; and cars used for drive hire, taxis and driving tuition, and including leasing costs as from 1 January 1994
- Business entertaining expenses
- Certain items bought for installation in new dwellings (such as fridges, washing machines)
- In the case of a company, the cost of providing domestic accommodation to a director or a person connected with a director.

Any purchases which relate partly to business use and partly to private use, for example home telephone charges, must be apportioned and only the proportion relating to business use reclaimed. However, Customs and Excise do not require car hire or car repair and maintenance expenses to be apportioned. Even if the vehicle is used substantially for private motoring, all input tax can be reclaimed. In addition, VAT can be reclaimed on all petrol and diesel used as fuel for a car, but a fixed amount must be accounted for on each VAT return for private use. The scale is fixed irrespective of the amount of private use (see Table 25, page 133).

Apart from the occasional low-value items where receipts cannot be obtained, for example telephone calls from call boxes, parking expenses etc, a tax invoice is required to support all VAT reclaims. The details required on a tax invoice are listed on page 128-29.

The following areas where VAT can be claimed are commonly overlooked:

- staff entertainment costs, for example a Christmas lunch
- subsistence expenses, for example meals away from place of business
- goods bought for gifts, for example bottles of wine at Christmas (but if the gift costs more than £15 output tax may be payable (see page 122)
- parking expenses (except parking meters which are not subject to VAT)
- telephone calls from call boxes
- leased equipment where payment is made by standing order.

It should be noted that whereas a separate VAT charge arises on each monthly or quarterly instalment under a straightforward leasing agreement, for VAT purposes a lease purchase agreement (a lease which gives the lessee an option to purchase the asset at the end of the lease) is treated as an outright sale, so that all the VAT is charged and, providing the asset is not a car, all may be reclaimed at the beginning of the lease period.

## *Subsistence expenses*

VAT can be reclaimed on subsistence expenses of the VAT registered person and his employees when they are away from their usual place of work on business. This includes all necessary expenses, for example hotel accommodation and meals, providing the cost is reimbursed by the business. If only part is reimbursed, then VAT is only reclaimable on that proportion. A tax invoice must be held.

Where a round sum allowance is paid to an employee, no VAT is reclaimable even if a tax invoice is obtained.

Where a person entertains while away on business, VAT can be claimed on the proportion of the cost of entertainment that relates to the taxable person or his employee. The proportion that relates to the guest is disallowed.

## *Mileage allowances*

VAT can be recovered on the fuel element of a mileage allowance. It is not necessary to hold the invoices. The VAT recoverable is likely to vary with the price of petrol, etc. It is often simpler therefore to agree with Customs an average amount of VAT recoverable on mileage allowances.

### **Imports and Exports**

## *Imports*

VAT is chargeable on the importation of goods into the UK. Two basic options are available to the business which has to pay VAT on goods imported from outside of the EC. Payment can either be made at the time of importation or can be deferred for an average of thirty days. Obviously the deferment option provides a cashflow benefit but Customs must be provided with a bank guarantee. The VAT charged on importation can then be recovered through the VAT return providing the appropriate certificate of import has been obtained from Customs.

Imports from countries within the EC are known as 'acquisitions'. In these circumstances the VAT is payable through the importer's VAT return. If the importer is fully taxable the VAT paid on the acquisition can be reclaimed through the same VAT return.

## *Exports*

The export of goods is zero rated providing Customs are satisfied that the goods have been exported. It is crucial, therefore, to obtain the required proof of export – within three months of the supply. Exports of goods to EC countries are known as 'dispatches' and the goods can only be zero rated if the exporter has obtained the customer's EC VAT registration number and holds the required proof of export.

A cashflow benefit can be obtained if a separate company is created to deal solely with the export of goods. This company can be placed on monthly VAT returns to recover VAT quickly, often before the manufacturer has accounted for VAT on the sale to the export company.

In addition to the above requirements, businesses which acquire or dispatch goods from or to the EC above certain limits will have to complete further returns in order to provide statistical information.

## Land and Buildings

The rules governing VAT on land, buildings and the supply of construction services are extremely complicated. The following is offered only as a brief outline; anyone buying, renting, selling, leasing or developing land or a building, or becoming involved in any other property transaction, is strongly urged to take professional advice before entering into any commitments. Similarly, building and civil engineering firms should take advice to ensure that the supplies they make are properly categorised. Failure to do so may result in tax being charged, which cannot be recovered, a penalty, or the loss of relief for tax suffered on purchases.

In general terms, the following supplies are now zero rated:

- The outright (freehold) sale of brand new houses, property converted into houses, flats and similar residential property
- The premium payable on the leasehold sale of such property, provided the lease is for more than 21 years
- A contractor's charges for building new houses and flats and converting property into housing.

Zero rating also applies to the construction and sale of certain other buildings, such as institutional residential accommodation (eg nursing homes) and property occupied by a charity for non-trading purposes (eg a building used for religious worship may be zero rated, but not a 'bring and buy' shop).

An important point to note is that work carried out by sub-contractors on buildings other than new houses and flats is standard rated, even if the main contractor's supply to the ultimate client is zero rated.

The following supplies are exempt:

- Sales of bare land
- Sales of residential property, unless brand new
- Sales of commercial or industrial buildings more than three years old
- Rents.

However, the owner of a non-residential building has the option to standard-rate what would otherwise be an exempt supply. This means that he must charge VAT to his purchaser or tenant, but may reclaim the VAT paid on the purchase or construction of the building. This 'election to waive exemption' or 'option to tax' is explained more fully below.

All supplies which are neither zero rated nor exempt are taxable at the standard rate. Thus 17.5 per cent must be charged on:

- The sale of newly constructed commercial and industrial buildings (those up to three years old)
- A contractor's charges for constructing buildings other than houses, flats, institutional residential accommodation and certain buildings used by charities
- A contractor's charges for alteration, repair or maintenance work (with some exceptions for residential listed buildings).

## *The option to tax*

As noted above, the owner of a non-residential building may elect to tax supplies which would otherwise be exempt. The election is made on a building-by-building basis and can also apply to discrete areas of agricultural land. Thus a developer may decide to tax all supplies in respect of a building he is refurbishing. This will enable him to reclaim the tax he pays on his refurbishment costs, but will oblige him to charge VAT on the premiums and rents paid by his tenants and on the eventual sale proceeds of the building. Once made, an option to tax can only be revoked during a short cooling off period or after 20 years (but the option will not bind any subsequent owner of the building). The decision whether or not to elect is thus of great importance and should be taken only after careful consideration.

The election to tax cannot be exercised retrospectively. If the landlord has previously made exempt supplies in respect of a building, he must obtain the permission of Customs and Excise in order to elect.

A tenant taking a new lease should bear in mind that VAT may be charged by the landlord on the rental.

## *Planning Points*

1. Businesses and charities who do not have full VAT recovery should consider placing property in a wholly owned property company.
2. It may be more cost effective to construct a new house, nursing home, hospice, etc, rather than enlarging an existing building. Demolition of an existing building is therefore a consideration.
3. The sale of a building within a period of ten years following its acquisition could create a VAT liability under the 'capital goods scheme' (see page 127).

Joint ventures should always consider potential VAT liabilities on services supplied between the venturers. A separate VAT registration of the parties involved is also a consideration.

## Partially Exempt Traders

As noted above, a trader who makes both taxable (standard rated or zero rated) and exempt supplies may only recover part of the tax he pays on his purchases. Such traders are known as 'partially exempt traders' and the general rule is that they must identify each purchase as being either:

- for the purposes of making taxable supplies; or
- for the purposes of making exempt supplies; or
- for the purpose of making both taxable and exempt supplies (for example, general overheads).

The trader may then reclaim as input tax the whole of the tax paid ('input tax') on items within the first category and a reasonable proportion of the tax on items in the last one. That proportion is normally arrived at by calculating as a percentage the ratio of taxable turnover to total turnover. If, for example, 40 per cent of turnover is taxable turnover, he will be allowed to reclaim 40 per cent of the input tax paid on his general overheads.

However, where the above method of calculating the input tax relief due would be impossible or cumbersome to operate, the trader may agree with Customs and Excise some other method of splitting purchases between taxable and exempt supplies.

Most importantly, the existence of exempt supplies may be ignored and associated input tax can be reclaimed in full if it is less than an average of £625 a month over a one-year period and less than 50 per cent of all input tax. This took effect in the VAT year starting April, May or June 1995; until then the limit was £600 per month, with no 5 per cent restriction.

## Capital goods scheme

A trader might buy a capital asset, temporarily use it for the purpose of making taxable supplies (so that he could reclaim the input tax paid) and then redeploy that asset to the making of exempt supplies. The 'capital goods scheme' was introduced in April 1990 to counter a perceived abuse of the rules. The scheme applies only to computers (and computer equipment) costing £50,000 or more and to buildings costing £250,000 or more (in both cases excluding VAT).

If a computer is redeployed to use in an exempt business, within five years of purchase, the original input tax relief claim is recalculated, to restrict the original VAT recovery on a pro rata basis.

A particular danger arises if a building is acquired with the addition of VAT and some time in the following ten years the purchaser sells the building free of tax. In these circumstances Customs and Excise would recover a proportion of the VAT incurred on its acquisition.

## Bad Debt Relief

Traders who have opted to use 'cash accounting' (see page 130) pay the

*128/Tax Facts*

VAT due on their sales only after it has been received from the customer. This scheme therefore gives automatic bad debt relief. If the customer does not pay, no VAT is due to Customs and Excise on the sale.

Generally speaking, traders using one of the nine special schemes for retailers (see page 129) also pay the VAT due on their sales only as they themselves are paid by their customers. Any other trader, however, has to pay the VAT at the end of the quarter in which the sale was invoiced, even if he is not paid by his customer until much later.

Bad debt relief in respect of VAT is available in respect of debts that are at least six months old and which have been written off to a 'bad debt relief account'. In these circumstances the VAT originally paid can be reclaimed through a VAT return.

## Accounting Records

In most cases you should be able to adapt your normal accounting records to suit VAT. The following shows the minimum that must be kept.

### Sales

1. Tax invoices: These must be issued for all standard rated supplies to other taxable persons. In practice most businesses other than retailers will issue invoices for all supplies. A tax invoice must show the following details:

   - Name and address of supplier
   - An identifying number
   - The supplier's VAT registration number
   - Customer's name and address
   - Date
   - Type of supply, for example sale, hire, sale or return
   - Description of supply
   - Charge excluding VAT
   - Discount offered (if applicable)
   - VAT payable.

   Certain additional details should be shown for tax invoices issued to businesses in other member states of the EU. Where the value of the supply is £100 or less (including VAT), a less detailed invoice can be issued. This need show only:

   - Name and address of supplier
   - His VAT registration number
   - Date
   - Description
   - Charge including VAT

- Rate of VAT.
2. Record of supplies made: If invoices are issued for all supplies this will be just a summary of those invoices in the order they are issued. If not, it will be a record of goods/services supplied.
3. Exports: Proof that the goods have been exported – for example, certificate of shipment or proof of posting.
4. Bad Debt Relief Account: see above.

## Purchases

1. Purchase invoices: With minor exceptions, tax invoices must be held for all supplies on which VAT is to be reclaimed.
2. Record of purchases: A list of purchase invoices received.
3. Import documentation: Copies of import entries must be held.

## VAT Account

The VAT Account should show the total VAT due on sales, the VAT reclaimable on purchases etc, and the amount of VAT payable or reclaimable for the period covered by the return.

## Retention of records

You must retain certain records for a minimum of six years unless you have agreed a shorter period with Customs and Excise. This includes purchase invoices and copy sales invoices.

## Retail Schemes

'Retail schemes' provide a method by which retail businesses which do not issue invoices for all transactions can calculate the VAT payable on their sales.

There are nine retail schemes, some of which have authorised adaptations. Not all retailers qualify to use each scheme. The various schemes produce different results and have differing requirements as to the type of records required. If you are a retailer you should consider carefully all the schemes that are available to you, as otherwise you could pay more VAT than necessary.

One of the requirements of all retail schemes is that a daily record of gross takings is maintained. Under most of the schemes this provides the basis for calculating the VAT payable, so it is essential that it is accurate. Customs and Excise regularly challenge takings figures where they consider them to be unrealistic and will raise an assessment if they conclude that the takings have been under-recorded. If there is a drop in takings or profit margins, you should note any reason for this, for example a competitor opening up next door, in case your figures are subsequently challenged by a VAT officer.

The choice of retail scheme is with you, the trader, and Customs and Excise have no power to direct that a particular scheme should be used. They can, however, withdraw the use of a particular scheme.

Once a retail scheme is selected you must use it for at least one complete year. A change of scheme is allowed at the end of any complete year but Customs and Excise must be notified in advance. A new business is allowed to change schemes retrospectively up to the time it receives its first VAT visit, which usually takes place within 18 months of registration. After that time retrospective changes are only allowed for businesses which have a turnover below £300,000. The change can be backdated up to a maximum of six years but refunds will only be made if the amount exceeds £100 per annum.

## *Cash Accounting*

'Cash accounting' is an optional scheme which allows VAT to be accounted for on the basis of cash received and cash paid rather than on the basis of invoices issued and received.

To be eligible to use the scheme you must meet the following conditions:

- Your annual taxable turnover excluding VAT must not exceed £350,000 ('taxable turnover' excludes any exempt income but includes zero rated sales)
- Your VAT returns must be up-to-date and you must owe Customs no more than £5,000
- You must not have been convicted of a VAT offence or assessed for dishonest conduct within the previous three years
- You must agree to comply with any conditions laid down by Customs and Excise.

### *Advantages*

The main benefits of the scheme are that:

- a business will not have to account for the VAT on its sales until it receives payment for them; and
- if payment is never received, there is no six-month waiting period for bad debt relief (see page 128).

However, a business will not be entitled to claim credit for the VAT on its purchases until it pays for them.

The main types of business that will benefit from the scheme are non-retail businesses which pay VAT on a regular basis. Under the normal rules, retail businesses will account for VAT on sales on a cash received basis anyway by using a retail scheme (see page 129) and so they are likely to be worse off under cash accounting as they will lose their entitlement to reclaim VAT on purchases as soon as they receive the invoice. Repayment businesses are also likely to be worse off.

A new business may be at a temporary disadvantage if VAT is being incurred on purchases of capital equipment or stock which is not claimable until the goods are paid for. In such cases, it would be advisable to wait until all the VAT on the major purchases has been reclaimed before adopting the cash accounting scheme.

## Records

Originally, the record-keeping requirements were quite onerous. However, all that need now be kept is a cashbook cross-referenced to purchase invoices and copy sales invoices (ie each invoice must be numbered and that number written in the cashbook).

If a purchase is paid for in cash (rather than by cheque or credit card) a dated receipt must be obtained.

## Ceasing to use the scheme

1. Compulsorily: The scheme has a 25 per cent tolerance limit – it can therefore be used until you reach a turnover of £437,500. If your turnover has exceeded this limit, or you expect it to exceed this in the next twelve months, you must notify Customs and Excise within thirty days.

    You will be required to leave the scheme at the beginning of the next VAT period.

    You will also be required to leave the scheme if you become subject to a default surcharge or other penalty.

2. Voluntarily: If you have used the scheme for at least two years and wish to leave, you can do so at the end of any complete year of use.

# Annual Accounting

'Annual accounting' is an optional scheme. It allows VAT to be accounted for by nine estimated payments during the year with one annual return being completed at the end of the year when the final payment is due.

Under this scheme you will have to accept Customs and Excise's estimate of the tax payable for the coming year. This estimate will be divided by ten and this amount will be the monthly payment for nine months. Payments will start in the fourth month of the year and must be made by direct debit. The return must be submitted within two months of the year-end with the tenth and balancing payment.

To be eligible to use the scheme you must meet the following conditions:

- You must have been registered for VAT for at least one year
- Your annual taxable turnover, excluding VAT, must be no more than £300,000 (excluding any exempt income)
- Your VAT returns and payments must be up to date
- You must not have claimed regular repayments in the year prior to application
- You must not be registered as part of a group or division of a company
- You must agree to comply with any conditions laid down by Customs and Excise.

## Advantages

The main benefit of the scheme is that only one return has to be rendered and two months are allowed in which to complete it.

If, however, your turnover decreases or increases in the year this could cause difficulties. If the turnover drops you may find it difficult to meet the payment (but you could then apply to leave the scheme immediately). If it increases you will be paying too little and the final payment at the end of the year could be substantial.

## Application

Annual accounting is allowed only where a written application has been made and approved by Customs and Excise. Application forms are available from your local VAT office.

## Ceasing to use the scheme

1. Compulsorily: You will be required to leave the scheme if you fail to make any of the monthly payments on time or at all, or you fail to submit the annual return by the due date. You will also be required to leave the scheme if your turnover exceeds £375,000. (This is the annual accounting turnover limit of £300,000 plus a tolerance of 25 per cent.) You will revert to quarterly accounting from the start of the next year.

2. Voluntarily: You can leave the scheme at any time. You should write to Customs and Excise and ask to revert to normal accounting.

## Private Petrol Benefit

Customs and Excise assess the private use of a company car by an individual by making a scale charge for the use of the car on a similar basis to income tax. These charges are shown in Table 25.

Table 25 *The VAT charges for the private use of company cars*

|  |  | Petrol | | Diesel | |
|---|---|---|---|---|---|
|  | Cylinder capacity | Scale charge | VAT payable | Scale charge | VAT payable |
| **Quarterly returns** | Up to 1,400cc | £177.00 | £26.36 | £160.00 | £23.82 |
|  | 1,401 – 2,000cc | £222.00 | £33.06 | £160.00 | £23.82 |
|  | Over 2,000cc | £330.00 | £49.14 | £205.00 | £30.53 |
| **Monthly returns** | Up to 1,400cc | £59.00 | £8.78 | £53.00 | £7.89 |
|  | 1,401 – 2,000cc | £74.00 | £11.02 | £53.00 | £7.89 |
|  | Over 2,000cc | £110.00 | £16.38 | £68.00 | £10.12 |

Note
The scale only applies to cars.

## Administration

### Returns

Once you are registered for VAT you will be allocated VAT return periods. Unless repayments are to be claimed regularly and monthly returns requested, quarterly return periods will be allocated. These will be chosen by Customs and Excise unless you request specific quarters.

The first return will not necessarily be for three months. Return forms are sent out by Customs and Excise shortly before the end of the quarter. They must be completed and returned to Customs and Excise within one month of the end of the return period, for example the return for the quarter to 31 December 1995 must be received by Customs and Excise no later than 31 January 1996 – it would not be sufficient to post the return on 31 January.

The return should show:

- the total VAT charged to your customers in the period
- the amounts of VAT charged by your suppliers in the period and
- the difference between the two.

The difference will be the amount payable to Customs and Excise, or the amount repayable by them.

For statistical and checking purposes, the return also asks the trader to state his total purchases and sales for the period and his total purchases from, and sales to, EC countries.

If there is an amount payable the return should be accompanied by a cheque, or alternatively arrangements can be made to make payments by credit transfer if more convenient. Customs and Excise prefer payments by credit transfer and will allow you an extra seven days in which to make payments and submit returns if you adopt this method. Failure to submit the return and/or the payment within the time allowed can result in penalties being imposed (see 'Penalties' page 136). Large payers of VAT (over £2 million per annum) have to make monthly payments but submit returns quarterly.

If there is an amount repayable by Customs and Excise, they will repay this amount to you, either directly to your bank or by cheque. A repayment will normally be made within thirty days of receipt of the claim unless extra time is needed to check its validity. If the repayment is not made within the time limit allowed then, provided the return is accurate to within £250 (or 5 per cent of the amount actually due, if greater) and was submitted by the due date, a supplement of 5 per cent is paid. This is payable in full, irrespective of the number of days by which the time limit was exceeded.

If returns will show repayments on a regular basis, you can request monthly returns. This will mean three times as many returns to be completed but could substantially aid cashflow.

## Late submission

If your VAT return is not received by the due date, Customs and Excise will estimate the amount of VAT payable by you for the quarter and issue an assessment. The amount of the assessment is enforceable by law. There is no right of appeal against an assessment unless a return has been submitted for the period concerned. The assessment will be cancelled automatically when the return is received.

The law provides for penalties to be imposed where returns are not received or are received after the due date.

If there is a particular reason why you cannot submit a return by the due date, for example illness, it is advisable to contact your local VAT office explaining the difficulty. This may assist if a penalty is imposed and you want to appeal against it. In exceptional circumstances Customs and Excise will allow the return to be estimated.

## Mistakes

The procedure for correcting errors on returns already submitted depends on the amount of tax involved. If correcting all the errors discovered results in an underpayment or overpayment of £2,000 or less, the trader may correct the position himself by adjusting the figure for output or input tax on the next return he submits.

However, if the net underpayment or overpayment is more than £2,000, the trader should make a voluntary disclosure to Customs and Excise. Interest is charged on notified underpayments.

If an underpayment is not disclosed by the trader but discovered by Customs (eg during an inspection visit), a 'misdeclaration penalty' may be charged (see page 137).

## Planning Points

1. VAT periods are not mandatory. If sales peak in a particular month, a cashflow benefit will be obtained if this month is the first month of the VAT quarter.
2. Consider payment by credit transfer if significant amounts of VAT are payable.

## Notifying Changes

If there are any changes, for example, a change of address or a change of bank account, you should write immediately to your local VAT office. This office will be shown on your 'certificate of registration' for VAT. You should not write to the VAT Central Unit nor should you wait until your next return is due. It is not advisable to include any correspondence with your return. If you claim repayments, it is particularly important to have changes dealt with before a return is due, as any repayment will be held up until the computer has updated your particulars.

### Registration numbers

Where there is a change in the legal status of your business, for example, if as a sole proprietor you take in a partner, you will be required to register for VAT and complete a new application form. You may be allowed to retain your existing VAT number if preferred. You will not be forced to keep the old number if you would prefer a new one. Usually, of course, it will be more convenient to keep the old VAT number. However, traders should note that if the old number is retained, the new proprietor(s) will take over all the outstanding VAT liabilities of the old.

A change other than a change of legal status will not affect your VAT number. You will, however, be issued with a new certificate of registration for VAT which will show your amended details.

### Sale of business

If you sell your business you should notify your local VAT office within thirty days. If the whole of your business is sold and you are not taking on another, your VAT registration will either be cancelled or transferred to the new owner (if you both agree).

If your business is sold as a going concern you will probably not have to charge VAT on the sale. VAT is not chargeable if:

- the assets are to be used in the same type of business; and
- the business was a going concern at the time of transfer; and
- the new owner is registered for VAT or becomes liable to be registered for VAT at the time of the transfer; and

- if only part of the business is sold, that part is capable of separate operation.

If the above applies, you must not charge VAT. However, it is wise to ensure that the contract of sale allows VAT to be added if Customs and Excise later prove not to be satisfied that the conditions were fulfilled.

A particular problem has developed when a business is sold which includes land and property where the option to tax (see page 125) has been exercised. In these circumstances it is recommended that professional advice is sought.

## Drop in turnover or business closure

If your turnover drops below the VAT registration limit, you are entitled to remain VAT registered if you wish. If you want your registration cancelled you must write to your local VAT office. You must be able to satisfy them that in the next twelve months your turnover will not exceed the cancellation limit, which is always slightly lower than the registration threshold and is currently £45,000, excluding VAT.

You should not stop charging VAT until Customs have agreed that your registration will be cancelled. They will advise you of the date from which you are no longer registered.

You will be required to submit a final return to the date of cancellation of the registration or of business closure.

If you close down your business, or cancel your registration on the grounds of reduced turnover, you will have to account for VAT on any business assets or stock if the VAT on them exceeds £250. This has to be included on your final return. It should be remembered that land and property are business assets.

## Penalties

In 1985 most VAT offences were decriminalised and a series of automatic 'civil penalties' introduced. Brief details of these are given below.

### 1. Late notification of liability to be registered

This penalty applies to taxpayers who do not notify their liability to be registered within the required thirty days. The penalty is calculated as a percentage of the tax due for the period beginning on the day the trader should have registered and ending on the day Customs and Excise received his notification that he should be registered. Subject to a fixed minimum penalty of £50 the current penalty rates are as follows:

| | |
|---|---|
| • registration no more than nine months late | 5 per cent |
| • registration over nine months late but no more than eighteen months late | 10 per cent |
| • registration over eighteen months late | 15 per cent |

The only defence is 'reasonable excuse'. Customs and Excise or a VAT tribunal can reduce the penalty to nil.

A point to watch is that a penalty may arise on a change of proprietor as well as on the commencement of a completely new business. For example, if a trader takes his son into partnership, the partnership must notify its liability to be registered (see page 118) and if it fails to do so within thirty days, a penalty may be charged.

## 2. Default surcharge

Taxpayers who do not submit returns by the due date will be liable for 'default surcharge'. It works as follows:

1. A return which is not received by the due date is recorded as a 'default' and a surcharge liability notice (SLN) is issued, warning that further 'defaults' within twelve months will be surcharged.
2. A second default within twelve months will attract a penalty of 2 per cent of the net tax due.
3. If a third 'default' is recorded within twelve months of the second, a penalty of 5 per cent of the tax payable on that return (or £30 if greater) is imposed. The duration of the SLN is extended.
4. If further 'defaults' are recorded the penalty increases in 5 per cent stages to a maximum of 15 per cent of the tax.
5. To escape from the surcharge routine twelve months' VAT payments must be made by the due date.

The penalty is not imposed if Customs and Excise are satisfied there is a 'reasonable excuse' for the 'default'.

## 3. Misdeclaration penalty

This penalty applies to errors, discovered by VAT officers, which exceed a certain level, being the lesser of:
— 30 per cent of the gross amount of tax, or
— £1 million.

The gross amount of tax is the aggregate of both the output tax and the input tax. The amount of the penalty is 15 per cent of the error.

The penalty is not imposed if there is a 'reasonable excuse' or if the trader corrects his error before it is discovered by Customs and Excise. The penalty can also be reduced by Customs and Excise to nil.

## 4. Default interest

Default interest is levied where an underpayment or overclaim has been made or where an assessment has been paid which is too low. The rate of interest is set by the Treasury to be broadly in line with commercial rates. This interest is not an allowable expense in computing profits for income or corporation tax purposes. Default interest will not be levied for a period greater than the last three years.

5. *Breaches of the regulations*

A penalty is applied to breaches of the regulations, for example failure to notify a cessation of trade, or failure to keep or produce records. The current penalties are as follows:

| | |
|---|---|
| Failure to preserve records for six years | £500 |
| Most other breaches | £5 per day for a first offence |
| | £10 per day for a second offence |
| | £15 per day for a third offence |

There is a minimum penalty of £50 and a maximum of 100 days at the appropriate rate. Except in the case of a failure to preserve records or to notify a cessation of trade, a written warning must be given before a penalty is applied.

*Reasonable excuse*

There is no definition of 'reasonable excuse' but the law states that the following are not reasonable excuses:

- insufficiency of funds
- reliance on a third party to perform any task.

What does constitute 'reasonable excuse' appears to vary depending on the exact circumstances. However, the trader will be expected to take all practical steps towards fulfilling his VAT obligations and it is not therefore advisable to rely on being able to avoid a penalty by claiming a reasonable excuse.

If Customs and Excise do not accept a reasonable excuse it is possible to appeal to a VAT tribunal.

## *Visits and Disputes*

VAT is a self-assessed tax. Customs and Excise therefore sends its officers out to check that the trader is calculating it correctly. All VAT registered businesses are visited by VAT officers although the frequency will vary from business to business depending on size and complexity, and to some extent compliance history.

VAT officers' rights: The VAT officer has the following basic rights and powers:

- To enter premises used in connection with the carrying on of a business at any reasonable time, and inspect those premises
- To inspect the records of the business and to ask for information on all aspects of the business.

*Visits*

A VAT officer will normally contact you by telephone to arrange a suitable date. If the date he suggests is inconvenient do not be afraid to say so as he will probably be quite happy to set a different date. Do not forget to make a note of the VAT officer's name and telephone number in case you need to contact him before a visit, for example if you find you can no longer keep the appointment. It is also courteous to give as much notice as possible as he will need to rearrange his schedule. You or the person in charge of the business should be present, as well as the bookkeeper who completes the VAT returns, since the VAT officer may ask questions that the bookkeeper cannot answer.

The VAT officer will want to discuss the business with you and to examine your accounting records to ensure VAT is correctly brought to account. He will be looking to see that all business activities have been included and that the returns rendered are credible in the light of what he has seen. He will not necessarily look at all aspects of your business. If there are any areas of concern you should ask him. If any rulings are given you should ask for confirmation in writing. Although VAT officers will try to be as helpful as possible, they cannot be expected to act as unpaid tax advisers, nor will they give an impartial view. Any rulings given will be only the Customs and Excise interpretation of the law.

## Reaching agreement

After he has examined your records the VAT officer will point out any areas about which he is not satisfied. You may agree on some points, though perhaps not all. Unless it is a very simple point, it is always advisable for you to insist that the VAT officer puts his contentions in writing. If he believes you have underpaid, he will raise an assessment, or if you have overpaid, a notice of the overpayment will be issued. He may withhold his assessment if there are any points which need clarifying. A letter requesting further information will normally give a time limit and as far as possible this should be met. If this is impossible, an interim reply should be sent explaining the delay. Once the areas of dispute have been considered a reply should be sent answering his contentions. It may be advisable to seek professional advice before replying.

On receiving your reply to any queries, the VAT officer will decide whether he should proceed with issuing the assessment. If he does, you will be required to pay it within thirty days unless you have asked for a review and the VAT office has agreed to withhold enforcement action.

## Challenging assessments

From the date of the assessment you have thirty days in which to appeal to a VAT tribunal. In most cases, however, it will be preferable to have Customs and Excise review the assessment first, in the hope of reaching an agreement without going on to a tribunal.

If you decide to ask for a review, you should write to Customs and Excise stating your grounds. When acknowledging your letter, Customs and Excise will confirm that the time limit for appealing to a tribunal will be extended to a certain date (or to a date to be specified in a later letter).

However, it is important that you either appeal, or have Customs' confirmation that an extension will be allowed, within the original thirty-day time limit.

A review will normally be carried out by an officer of a higher grade and may involve him visiting you to discuss the problem or examine your records. You will be advised in writing of the outcome of the review.

## *Challenging decisions or penalties*

Again you have thirty days from the date of the letter containing the disputed decision, or of the notification of a penalty, in which to appeal or ask for a review. Further action should be taken as with assessments.

## *Further action*

If you are dissatisfied with an assessment or ruling, it is wise to seek professional advice in reviewing it. The VAT officer will be more knowledgeable about VAT than you are and you may not be able to counter his contentions effectively.

If a review results in an assessment being upheld and you wish to proceed to a tribunal, it is essential to seek professional assistance. It is permitted for the taxpayer to present his own case at the tribunal, but as Customs and Excise will be represented by an experienced officer (or possibly a solicitor or barrister), they will be able to present their case much more forcefully. Appeals where the taxpayer is professionally represented have a much higher success rate. Accountants as well as solicitors and barristers may represent clients before a VAT tribunal.

# 9

# Stamp Duty

Stamp duty, first imposed over 300 years ago in 1694, is the oldest tax levied. The system was consolidated into the Stamp Act 1891 which is still today's basis of charge. Stamp duty is paid by the purchaser in certain transactions, on 'instruments', and is a tax on documents, which means that there is only stamp duty when a transaction is effected in writing. There are specific 'heads of charge', some subject to exempt limits, and only documents within these heads are dutiable. A complete exemption from the charge arises where the documents are executed outside the UK and do not relate to UK property. There are numerous exemptions and since March 1985 instruments which effect a gift are not liable to stamp duty.

The main sanction for not stamping a dutiable document is that it is not admissible in civil proceedings. This means that without stamping, share transfers cannot be registered, transfers of registered land cannot be registered, and conveyances of land do not give 'good title', ie are not valid.

Failure to stamp at the proper time can be remedied by presenting the document to the Stamp Office and paying a penalty in addition to any stamp duty.

Table 26 *Stamp duty on conveyances and sales*

| Instrument | Rate of tax | Exempt limit |
|---|---|---|
| Stock transfer, Purchase by company of own shares, Letters of allotment and Takeovers and mergers | 0.5% | N/A |
| Conversion of shares into depository receipts | 1.5% | N/A |
| Property conveyance or transfer on sale | 1% | £60,000 |

# Tax Facts

The duty payable in respect of leases is calculated on a sliding scale which takes into account the duration of leases and the average rent and is based on a percentage of that rent. Where the rent exceeds £500 per annum, it is as follows (for each £50 or part thereof):

| | |
|---|---|
| Less than seven years or indefinite term | 1 per cent |
| 7–35 years | 2 per cent |
| 35–100 years | 12 per cent |
| Over 100 years | 24 per cent |

The Stock Exchange is due to introduce paperless share transfers under the CREST system and as stamp duty is a tax on documents the rules are changing. The changes occur on 1 July 1996 when a stamp duty reserve tax is introduced. The rate of tax is the same as for stamp duty (0.5 per cent).

# 10

# Tax Planning

Overview — Income tax — Corporation tax — Capital gains tax — Inheritance tax

## Overview

Since 6 April 1988 capital gains have been taxed as though they were the highest part of an individual's income. Therefore, capital gains are taxed at the same rate as income, for individuals as well as companies. It is true that in many cases the rebasing of capital gains together with the indexation allowance and the annual capital gains tax exemption, will still result in the tax payable on capital gains being lower than would be the case for income. There are situations where it is better to obtain income rather than capital gains. Two examples are:

1. Income can be sheltered by investing in Enterprise Investment Schemes and Venture Capital Trusts (see Chapter 2) or 'enterprise zone' properties. This may reduce the rate of tax payable on capital gains. Investment in an enterprise zone, for example, attracts a 100 per cent industrial buildings allowance (see pages 73-5).

2. When shares in a private company are being sold, there is often a tax advantage to a shareholder if he receives a dividend before disposing of his shareholding for a correspondingly lower sum.

## Income Tax

### Home Purchases

Multiple income tax relief: Where two or more taxpayers took out mortgages prior to 1 August 1988, to buy one home to share, each taxpayer receives interest relief, at 15 per cent from 6 April 1995, on the first £30,000 of his mortgage. Care must be taken if any changes are made in these circumstances, such as the refinancing of mortgages, as this is likely to lead to a loss of interest relief, because relief is currently limited to interest on £30,000 per residence.

Interest relief: If you are thinking of buying a house or moving, you should consider arranging your borrowing in such a way that tax relief is obtained on interest payments, whenever possible. However with relief now given at only 15 per cent from 6 April 1995, coupled with the currently lower rates of interest receivable on investments, the tax advantages of this type of borrowing have been substantially reduced so that borrowing up to £30,000 for house purchase is no longer always sensible where you have available funds. It may still be beneficial to consider increasing your mortgage on moving to the maximum amount qualifying for tax relief (£30,000) since this may release capital which can be used for other purposes on which no tax relief is available, for example paying school fees or buying a new car.

You must ensure the borrowing is set up correctly. Interest paid on an overdraft, used for the same purpose, will not qualify for tax relief.

If you need a short-term 'bridging loan' when moving house, you can obtain tax relief on a loan of up to £30,000 for 12 months – and sometimes even longer with the Inland Revenue's approval.

In appropriate circumstances, you could consider pension-linked mortgages, which can be useful tax-efficient ways of providing capital repayment. A recent innovation is the PEP mortgage, linked to a personal equity plan (see page 29).

## *Employee Share Schemes*

An employee can acquire shares, or an option to acquire shares, without any income tax charge arising, and without a capital gains tax charge arising until he disposes of his shares. This means that share schemes can be offered to employees, which attract Inland Revenue approval, in the knowledge that no employee will pay tax on his shares until he disposes of them. (See pages 61-2.)

## *Tax Repayments*

Many people who only have a small income and receive this in part from bank and building society interest now have to reclaim any excess tax paid, because that income is taxed at 24 per cent, whereas they are liable only to 20 per cent tax on the first £3,900 of income.

This applies in 1995/96. However, in 1996/97 income from bank and building societies will only be subject to tax deductions at 20 per cent.

## *Husband and Wife*

Husbands and wives are taxed as separate individuals, for all sources of income and gains. Each spouse is entitled to a personal allowance and to have the first £3,900 of taxable income taxed at 20 per cent and next £21,600 at 24 per cent. Consequently, it may be beneficial to transfer a source of income or an asset with a large potential capital gain to the spouse with the lower rate of tax. However, any such transfer will only be tax effective if beneficial ownership of the asset giving rise to the income or gain (see Chapter 7) is transferred. It is not sufficient, for example, for a man to set up a trust under which the income produced by the trust assets is paid to his wife, while he retains control of the capital. Indeed, the creation of such a trust could precipitate a taxable gain on the husband. If one spouse is not paying tax, consider transferring investments which can provide gross income. Similarly, consider an election to re-allocate jointly held investments, not held in equal shares, if it results in more income being taxed at lower rates.

Within a family business it may be worthwhile increasing the remuneration of the spouse if this can be justified in commercial terms, to utilise the spouse's personal allowance and lower rates of income tax.

## *Children's Investments*

If your minor children (under 18) do not use all their personal allowances and have surplus cash, their investments should be carefully planned. Investments which pay interest gross should be put first on the list of possible investments. These include the National Savings Bank, certain other National Savings products, and bank and building society accounts, provided the appropriate declaration as to your children's tax status is lodged with the institution. If any UK income tax is deducted from investment income arising to minor children in the current tax year, depending on their other income, they may be able to reclaim that tax.

## *Other Interest Relief*

If you need to borrow for purposes other than house purchase, you should always consider in advance the possibility of obtaining tax relief, which is not available on overdrafts, but may be on other borrowings. Savings can be obtained in appropriate circumstances. This particularly applies to money borrowed to buy a share in, or make a loan to, a partnership, or to buy shares in a close company. In each case various conditions have to be satisfied to obtain tax relief. Tax relief on such loans can be at your highest rate of income tax, compared to the now limited relief given on house purchase loans.

## *Retirement*

If you are retired or are contemplating retirement and are concerned that you will have insufficient income, you may find that it is possible to raise funds by mortgaging your house and purchasing an annuity with the proceeds. Your spendable income will increase but you will have less capital to leave to your dependants. It will not normally be advantageous unless you are at least 70 years old, but much depends upon your personal circumstances. As the various schemes available and annuity rates differ significantly, it is important to take independent advice.

## *Company Cars*

If your employer makes a car available to you for your private use, you will normally be taxed on a deemed benefit in kind, calculated by reference to the list price (see Table 13). In addition, the National Insurance liability for employers is based on both the car benefit and on the private fuel scale charge (see Table 17). These rules apply to employees earning in excess of £8,500 inclusive of benefits and to all directors. All companies and employees with company cars need to review their position as, at no extra cost to the employer, the employee can buy their own car and be paid a higher salary and a mileage allowance, which could be based on either the AA mileage rates or those set by the Inland Revenue under the Fixed Profit Car Scheme. This latter scheme does not pay such high rates as the AA mileage rates. However, the Fixed Profit Car Scheme mileage payments are not subject to income tax, whereas all other mileage payments are subject to income tax where the reimbursements exceed the costs of the taxpayer's business mileage.

The advantages of having a company car are rapidly disappearing. However, there are ways of reducing the tax burden. If your business mileage is more than 2,500 in a tax year to 5 April the benefit will be reduced by one third. On the other hand, the benefit will be reduced by two thirds if your business mileage is 18,000 or more. It is therefore worth while reviewing business mileage covered towards the end of the tax year to see whether planned business trips should be brought forward, so that the scale charge is minimised.

As mentioned above, a scale charge will arise if your employer pays for your private fuel. If you reimburse your employer for the cost of all fuel used for private purposes, the car fuel charge will not apply. In some cases, if private use is low, it is better to pay for all private petrol personally so that the car fuel charge is avoided. Generally, this arrangement needs to be in place from 6 April, to be effective.

The employer's national insurance contribution will be based on the Inland Revenue car benefit and car fuel scales. You should keep records of your business mileage to be able to substantiate a claim for a lower scale charge based on mileage claimed. In discussion about the collection of the new National Insurance charge, the DSS has said that it will accept mileage details supplied to the Inland Revenue on forms

P11D. Adequate records should also be kept to show that you have paid for all private fuel. Normally, travelling between home and office, or factory, is regarded as private use for car and car fuel benefit purposes. If you have to make a payment for the use of the car, as a condition of its being available for your private use, the taxable benefit can be correspondingly reduced. This does not include a contribution toward private petrol. If you have to make a payment for the use of the car, make sure that it is clearly described as being for its use and not for private petrol, as a partial payment for private fuel will not reduce the car fuel scale charge.

## Mobile Phones

A benefit in kind arises on the private use of mobile telephones provided by employers. Income tax is paid on the standard amount of £200 for all mobile telephones – including those fixed in cars. Short of reimbursing the full cost (including annual value but not rental) of all private calls, the only way to escape the charge is not to make any, and to prove that none are made; a full record of all calls must be kept for presentation to the Inspector of Taxes.

## Interest-free Loans

A small interest-free loan can be a useful tax-free benefit for employees such as helping to fund season ticket loans for home to work travel. A tax charge will only arise on the loans to the extent that the loan exceeds £5,000. This is in addition to loans which already qualify for tax relief – such as those within the £30,000 limit for the purchase of a home.

Great care must be taken where a company owned by the directors or by a small group of people, such as a family, is contemplating making a loan to a director or shareholder, as further tax liabilities can arise. For example, a loan to a shareholding director would be treated as a distribution by the company, and an amount equivalent to advance corporation tax would have to be accounted for. This advance corporation tax would only be refunded when the loan was repaid.

## In-house Services for Employees

Services such as travel, building services or schooling provided in-house are taxed on the marginal cost to the employer, which can be substantially lower than full cost.

## Award Schemes for Employees

Award schemes for staff or customers may increase business profits. They are also tax efficient since prizes up to £5,000 from a staff suggestion scheme can be tax-free.

## Speeding Tax Relief

The quickest way to obtain tax relief, for those taxed within the PAYE system, is via the notice of coding. Thus, if your personal circumstances change during a year and you are eligible for extra allowances, it is essential that you inform your Inspector of Taxes so that the change can be incorporated in that year's notice of coding, rather than waiting until after the end of the tax year to make a repayment claim.

## Unquoted Trading Companies

If you incur a capital loss on the disposal of ordinary shares you subscribed for in a qualifying trading company, then instead of claiming capital gains tax relief on the loss (at up to 40 per cent) it may be possible to claim income tax relief (also at up to 40 per cent). A similar relief is available if a claim is made for such shares to be treated as worthless and the claim is accepted by the Inland Revenue.

## Offshore Currency Funds

Funds established outside the UK enable income and capital gains tax to be deferred until disposal of the investment or receipt of a distribution (dividend). Some funds – known as 'distributor' funds – distribute a large proportion of their income each year, and as such you will obtain no income tax advantage by investing in those funds. Other funds, however, 'roll up' their income, and if you invest in these you will pay no income tax until you realise your investment. If you can realise your investment in a year when you are not resident in the UK, or have a low level of income (for example after retirement) then you may receive the income at that stage with little or no income tax liability. Note that a switch between funds – for example, from an equity to a gilts fund – is counted as a disposal of the original investment, triggering the appropriate tax charge.

There is also a significant advantage with bonds, of which some of the more attractive are offshore bonds. It is possible to draw down up to 5 per cent a year tax free, so that in the present economic climate of low rates of interest this can be extremely attractive. Bonds also possess the attraction that it may well be possible to switch investments within the bond without triggering a liability to capital gains tax until such time as the bond itself is encashed.

## Working Abroad

In some circumstances tax savings can arise if you are employed outside the UK for a complete tax year. If you are planning to work abroad, leave before 5 April rather than after so that you can meet this qualification at the earliest opportunity, and in most circumstances it is better to return just after the end of the tax year rather than just before.

# Tax Planning/149

If you are employed abroad for 365 days or more and all your duties are performed outside the UK, your earnings should be free of UK tax regardless of your residence status. There is no marginal relief, so you should ensure the exemption is not lost for the sake of a few days. You can make a number of visits to the UK without losing the exemption.

If you have established yourself as resident and ordinarily resident outside the UK, you are normally exempt from capital gains tax while you are abroad. (There is an exception for gains connected with certain trading or professional activities in the UK.) It may be advantageous to use this period of non-residence to realise any capital gains on your assets free of UK tax, but care must be taken to ensure you do not incur overseas tax or crystallise a 'held-over' gain arising on assets gifted to you.

If you decide to work abroad, it is generally better to do so as an employee under a contract running for 365 days or more. This is because it is possible to establish that you are provisionally not resident in the United Kingdom from the day you leave, whereas people leaving without a 12-month contract of employment may have to wait for up to three years to establish that they are not resident in this country. This is less important if you are leaving the UK permanently with no intention of returning.

Although the rules governing whether or not you are treated as resident in the UK for tax purposes can be complex, it is possible to reduce substantially a UK tax bill by obtaining appropriate professional advice before action is taken.

## *Pension Schemes*

Membership of a company pension scheme, otherwise known as an occupational scheme, is a very tax-efficient long-term investment, provided the scheme has been approved by the Inland Revenue. Your contributions of up to 15 per cent of your salary are deducted from your salary before tax. Your employer can also make contributions on your behalf, subject to the overall funding requirements of the scheme.

The benefits provided by an occupational scheme are also subject to detailed Inland Revenue rules. The maximum entitlement will depend on a number of factors, such as:

- when you became a member of the scheme
- your length of service at the date of retirement; and
- the rules of the scheme.

Since 1989 an employer has been able to top up a scheme member's pension by making contributions to a funded unapproved retirement benefit scheme. Such schemes may in certain circumstances prove attractive, particularly in the period leading up to retirement, for although they are not as tax efficient as an approved scheme they are more flexible.

## Additional Voluntary Contributions (AVCs)

As mentioned above, employees who are members of an occupational pension scheme can obtain income tax relief on pension contributions of up to 15 per cent of their gross earnings. Although most approved pension plans have regular employee contributions, these are normally less than the 15 per cent maximum, so that employees have scope to make additional voluntary contributions (AVCs). These will increase the eventual benefits accruing to the employee on retirement and can be a tax-effective way of saving because the income of the pension fund is tax free. Your occupational pension scheme is required by law to provide you with the facility to make AVCs if appropriate. In addition, you may make AVCs outside your company pension scheme to any approved plan of your choice.

## Business profits

With the introduction of self-assessment, and the transitional arrangements for taxing business profits of partnerships and sole traders, transitional rules have been enacted covering the period up to 5 April 1997. The transitional rules are complex and professional advice is needed to ensure that the business is not adversely affected by these rules. A brief summary of the rules is given on page 66.

## Additional Routes

The following may be considered as routes to saving tax:

- private medical insurance premiums if over 60 years of age
- workplace nurseries
- TESSAs
- deeds of covenant
- payroll deduction schemes
- gift aid
- age allowance
- Enterprise Investment Scheme (also re-investment relief)
- Venture Capital Trusts
- Personal Equity Plans
- industrial buildings allowances in enterprise zones
- employee share option schemes
- profit-sharing schemes
- employee share ownership plans
- Profit-Related Pay
- personal pension schemes
- national savings certificates
- friendly society investments.

## Corporation Tax

A great deal of corporation tax planning revolves around the timing in the recognition of income for tax purposes and the timing of allowable expenditure. Where commercial considerations permit the following areas should be examined:

### *Deferral of Income*

1. Delaying sales until a later accounting period by selling on consignment.

2. Certain income, for example bank interest, is taxed only when received. Consider having such interest credited immediately after the end of an accounting period rather than within it.

3. Seasonal traders should consider whether the accounting date should be timed to end before a high point in the business cycle.

### *Acceleration of Expenditure*

1. Acceleration of revenue expenditure planned for next year, into the current year.

2. Interest payable to a lender other than a UK bank is generally allowed for tax purposes when it is to be paid. Consider arranging for such interest to be paid shortly before the end of an accounting period rather than shortly after.

3. Acceleration of capital expenditure qualifying for capital allowances planned for next year, into the current year. The capital expenditure need not be paid for by the year-end, provided payment is made within four months of the invoice date.

4. Review the adequacy of all reserves, for example for bad debts. Generally, reserves are tax deductible where a liability exists and it can be calculated with reasonable accuracy.

5. Ensure that all remuneration charged in the accounts is paid within nine months of the end of the accounting period.

6. Ensure pension contributions are paid before the end of the accounting period. Ordinary annual contributions are allowed when paid, whereas in certain circumstances relief for special contributions in excess of the ordinary annual contribution will be spread.

7. Consider whether all known and quantifiable liabilities have been provided for in accordance with proper, ongoing and prudent accounting principles.

## Other Planning Points

1. Where possible reduce the taxable profits to below the small companies limit. For the year ending 31 March 1997 the rate of corporation tax for a company with no associates will be 24 per cent on profits below £300,000, or 33 per cent if profits exceed £1,500,000. Profits falling between these limits will be taxed at an effective rate of 35.25 per cent. Consider paying bonuses to employees or directors to reduce profits falling within the 35.25 per cent tax margin.

2. Consider whether a dividend or bonus should be paid and the tax effect, bearing in mind that:

   i) A bonus may attract employee/employer NI liability whereas no NI liability arises on dividends.

   ii) Generally where a company pays tax at the 24 per cent corporation tax rate it will be less expensive to pay a dividend. Conversely it is generally better to pay a bonus rather than a dividend if the company is paying corporation tax at the marginal rate of 35.25 per cent or the full rate of 33 per cent.

   iii) Any loss arising as a result of a bonus payment may be carried back against profits arising in the previous three years and a corporation tax refund obtained. The advance corporation tax (ACT) on a dividend can, however, be carried back against tax paid in the previous six years.

3. i) Consider the timing of dividend payments. ACT is recoverable against the tax liability on profits in the year in which the dividend is paid. Consider whether the dividend should therefore be paid shortly before the end of the accounting period rather than shortly after.

   ii) During the accounting period, the quarterly system for ACT means that retiming the payment of a dividend from the end of one quarter to the beginning of the next one produces a three-month cashflow advantage in ACT payments.

4. Ensure the correct classification of capital expenditure qualifying for capital allowances. It is particularly important to identify plant in buildings when purchasing property or buildings, and plant and machinery used for scientific research which qualify for 100 per cent allowances.

5. Ensure the correct classification between repairs to and improvement of fixed assets. Repairs will generally be fully tax deductible whereas improvements will be regarded as capital – but may qualify for capital allowances. Consider making provision for known liabilities under maintenance contracts on an accruals basis.

6. Consider whether short-life assets (assets expected to be sold or scrapped within four years) should have capital claimed on them separately, in isolation from the main pool of assets purchased by the business. If such assets are sold for less than their tax written-down value, this will accelerate the allowances available.
7. Special rules apply to groups of companies and consideration should be given to the following planning points:
    i) The use of the management charges to reduce profits to the small companies rate of 24 per cent. Ensure that the management charges are commercially justifiable.
    ii) The use of group relief to surrender losses to save tax at the full or marginal rates of corporation tax.
    iii) Ensure that an election is made to enable dividends to be paid by subsidiaries to the parent without accounting for ACT. (Similarly an election can be made for inter-group interest payments to be made without accounting for income tax.)
    iv) If a group company has unutilised capital losses, consider transferring assets, upon which a capital gain will arise on sale outside the group, to the capital-loss company prior to sale.
    v) If a subsidiary is to be sold, consider paying a dividend out of distributable reserves prior to sale to reduce or eliminate the capital gain.
    vi) Consider whether tax can be saved by operating trades as a division rather than through subsidiaries.

## Capital Gains Tax

### *Rates of Capital Gains Tax*

Personal capital gains are now taxed at 20, 24 or 40 per cent. The rate of tax which will apply will depend on the amount of income received in the same year. It is therefore beneficial to arrange for gains to be made in years of low income rather than high income, to reduce the effective rate of tax. It is also worth ensuring that any assets for disposal are held by the spouse with the lower rate of tax and the greater balance of exemption.

### *Trusts and Capital Gains Tax*

Whereas individuals may pay tax on capital gains at a rate of up to 40 per cent, trusts normally pay tax at only 24 or 34 per cent, depending on their nature and unless the settlor has an interest in possession. This means that, if large capital growth is expected in the value of an asset, such as shares in a family company, there is likely to be a tax advantage if those shares are settled in trust while the value is still low.

### *Planning Sales*

You can make significant savings in capital gains tax if you plan carefully the sale of your assets.

Capital gains tax is assessed for fiscal years – years ended 5 April. The tax is payable after the end of the fiscal year in which the disposal is made. If an asset is sold on 5 April 1996 the tax is payable on 1 December 1996. If the same asset is sold on 6 April 1996 the tax assessed is for 1996/97, which will be under the new Self Assessment rules, and is payable on 31 January 1998. There is an increased time in which to pay the tax.

If you are selling an asset at a loss, try to ensure the disposal is made in a year in which you can make use of the loss, although losses can be carried forward indefinitely.

The annual capital gains tax exemption (£6,300 for 1996/97) allows you to realise some gains each year without incurring a tax charge. For married couples, each spouse is entitled to an exemption of £6,300 in the tax year to 5 April 1997. As transfers between husband and wife are tax free it will pay to transfer an asset to the spouse with an available exemption and with the lower rate of income tax, before the disposal is made. Care must be taken to ensure that any such transfer is a genuine transfer.

If you would like to sell investments to make use of the exemption, but still wish to retain them for future growth, the answer is often to dispose of and reacquire shares on consecutive days, ie 'bed and breakfast' them. You will find that the bank or stockbroker dealing with your investments is familiar with such transactions and should know what to do. It is important that it is done properly if it is to be effective for capital gains tax purposes.

Investments standing at a loss can be sold or bed and breakfasted to bring your capital gains for the year down to the annual exemption, and thus reduce or eliminate the capital gains tax payable for the year.

Indexation allowance may be used to reduce a gain. This allowance can be substantial where assets have been held for a long time and must always be taken into account for capital gains tax planning in relation to such assets.

For assets held at 31 March 1982 it is possible to elect to use the 31 March 1982 value instead of cost. This election must be made within a specified time limit and, once made, applies to all chargeable assets held which were acquired before 31 March 1982.

## Second Homes

If you have more than one home, consider which house would benefit from exemption from capital gains tax. Choose the house which you expect will show the largest capital gain and notify the Inland Revenue.

## Rollover and Retirement Reliefs

If business assets are given away, donor and donee may elect to defer any capital gains tax until the donee sells the assets. If the donor has worked full-time in the business, all or part of any gain may be covered by retirement relief. This latter relief is particularly important now that this is available from the age of 50 and no tax is payable on gains of up to £250,000 and tax is only levied at half the normal rate on gains on the next £750,000.

However, careful advance planning is necessary to make the most of these reliefs; for example, assets (such as business premises) held outside the company will qualify for retirement relief only if the company has not paid a rent for their use. Also, husband and wife are both entitled to claim retirement relief, so that the total relief available may be doubled by ensuring both spouses have substantial stakes in the business.

The extension of re-investment relief in recent years was particularly welcome as it enables any form of capital raised by sale, which would otherwise result in the payment of capital gains tax, to be introduced into a private company as share capital. The same principle of rollover has also been granted to Venture Capital Trusts where you may invest in a quoted company that specialises in making investments in unquoted companies. This enables you to spread the risk of investment, since the Venture Capital Trusts will hold a selection of investments in a variety of unquoted companies. In a similar manner, under the Enterprise Investment Scheme, it is now possible to roll over the gain against the issue of new shares in an unquoted company, in which the investor does not have a stake of over 30 per cent. Furthermore, it is possible that the new investor can become a paid director. In addition, under both Venture Capital Trusts and Enterprise Investment Schemes, the new investor can obtain relief at the lower rate of income tax of 20 per cent on investments of up to £100,000 per annum, as well as obtaining exemption from capital gains tax on the subsequent sale. While these reliefs are extremely attractive, because of the variety, their differing implications on income tax as well as capital gains tax means deciding how best to proceed can be complex and professional advice is often needed.

## Share Exchanges

If the proprietors agree to exchange their shares for shares in another company, no tax is payable until the replacement shares themselves are sold. This can be useful where a privately owned company is to be 'taken over' by a public company. The most important consideration is, of course, that the proprietors of the original company must be confident that the new shares they receive will hold their value and will be easy to sell when the time comes to do so. If the new shares are held until death, they will of course pass to the heirs free of capital gains tax (as explained in Chapter 6). Alternatively, small parcels of 'new' shares may be sold year by year, to utilise the vendor's annual capital gains tax exemption. It will also now be possible to use this method of deferral until such time as suitable opportunities arise to invest in Enterprise Investment Scheme companies or Venture Capital Trusts and the gain will be rolled on into these later investments, further postponing the payment of tax.

## Profits

Even if retirement relief is not available, and a share-for-share exchange is not appropriate, steps may still be taken to reduce the capital gains tax payable on the sale of a company. For example, value may be stripped out of the company, prior to sale, by means of special contributions to the directors' pension fund.

Particular difficulties may arise where shares are sold for an immediate cash payment plus a promise of further payments if specified performance targets are met (commonly referred to as 'earn-out agreements'), or where an agreed purchase price is payable by instalments. The problem in some such cases is that a capital gains tax liability based on the full projected receipts can arise at the outset, so that it is quite possible for the tax then payable to exceed the amount initially received.

The vendors may be able to reduce this difficulty by the use of a share-for-share exchange, or other appropriate arrangements, but the tax implications of an earn-out or sale by instalments should be borne in mind at an early stage of the sale negotiations. Earn-outs also commonly cause commercial problems. For example disputes may arise as to the true profit made by a company and therefore whether the earn-out target has been met.

## Business Assets Held Outside the Company

It will often be the case that business assets – particularly freehold premises – are held outside the company. If these are sold, the only relief available (when the company is also sold) will be retirement relief and even this will be reduced or eliminated if the company has paid a rent for their use. One possibility might be to retain ownership of the premises and simply lease them to the new proprietors of the company. Alternatively, it may be possible at least to reduce the tax payable by arranging for the shares and the freehold premises to be sold in separate tax years.

### Inheritance Tax

The most effective and appropriate arrangements to mitigate the effect of inheritance tax will vary with the circumstances of the case. Do not assume that inheritance tax will not apply to you. Anyone with a house, life assurance or pension benefits and other assets which exceed £200,000 in value is potentially liable to a tax of which the rate on death is 40 per cent.

## Lifetime Gifts

If you can afford to make lifetime gifts, try to ensure that they are potentially exempt transfers (which attract no tax if made more than seven years before death). Potentially exempt transfers have three important advantages even if death does occur within the seven-year risk period:

1. The charge on death is based on the value of the gift when made, which means that increases in value escape tax.
2. Tax is charged at the rates ruling at the date of death, which could be lower than those at the date of the gift.
3. Payment of tax is deferred until death and it may be possible to cover the liability by insurance.

## Accumulation and Maintenance Settlements

Particular consideration should be given to accumulation and maintenance settlements, which can combine the creation of life interests where the beneficiaries are under 25, with the trustees continuing to have discretion over capital.

## Seven-year Rule

As gifts are 'written-off' for inheritance tax purposes after seven years and are therefore disregarded in fixing the rate of tax on further gifts or on assets passing on death after this seven-year period has expired, tax can be saved by making gifts as early in life as practicable.

## Reservation of Benefit

When making lifetime gifts, you should try to ensure that there is no reservation of benefit, which will result in the asset being brought into charge on death.

## Exemptions

It is advisable to try to take advantage of the various exemptions, including the annual exemption of £3,000 available to both husband and wife. The annual or normal expenditure out of income exemption may usefully cover the payment of premiums on a life policy written in trust for the beneficiaries, or payments under deed of covenant.

## Business and Agricultural Property Relief

Care should be taken to maximise entitlement to the business and agricultural property reliefs. This is particularly important with the extension of the reliefs in 1992.

## Shares in Private Companies

In planning gifts of shares in private trading companies, the value of a gift is based on the loss to the donor rather than the value of what is received by the donee. The two values may be very different and specialist advice is vital.

In many cases the shares in an unquoted trading company, or a USM or AIM company, will be eligible for 100 per cent business property relief, if they are held for at least two years. The relief is extremely generous and means that private company shares are to all purposes outside the scope of inheritance tax. This relief may not continue indefinitely. Shareholders should consider their present holdings in private, USM and AIM companies. They need to decide whether to give parts of their holdings away to the next generation or whether to settle such holding into some form of trust for the benefit of their families. By breaking up their large holdings they may now reduce any future inheritance tax on their assets since the value of smaller holdings may be appreciably lower if tax is once again levied on private company shares. All shareholders in private companies should review their position before the next election.

The present business property relief given against the value of shares in unquoted companies means that at present it may be possible to pass shares down to the next generation with a minimum of tax consequences. In family businesses it is thus possible to minimise the impact of inheritance tax. There will be increasing opportunities to invest directly in small unquoted companies as a result of the growing importance of the Enterprise Investment Scheme and re-investment relief. It should be noted that such investments (unlike Venture Capital Trusts) will qualify for business property relief at the rate of 100 per cent in most cases, as opposed to quoted investments which are taxed at their full value. This additional tax break may be important to certain taxpayers. It is important to carefully consider the additional risks that arise from direct investment in unquoted companies.

## Wills and the Nil Rate Band

Wills should be reviewed regularly to ensure that they are still appropriate to current circumstances. As husband and wife each have the benefit of a nil rate band, it is advisable to try to ensure as far as possible that assets equal to at least the nil rate band pass to the children or to a family trust on the first death. If necessary, lifetime gifts may be made between the spouses, so as to enable the recipient to make further gifts by will and during their lifetime.

## Insurance

Insurance still has a role to play in inheritance tax planning, either to cover the possibility of a premature death or to build up a fund outside the estate. Death in service benefits should also be placed in trusts outside the estate of the individual concerned.

## Assets that will Increase in Value

It is sensible to try to give away assets which are likely to increase in value (eg freeholds), and retain those which are likely to depreciate (eg short leases).

## Retaining Flexibility

When considering inheritance tax arrangements, take account of the effect of other taxes, especially capital gains tax and income tax. Retain flexibility to meet changing personal, financial and taxation circumstances. Inheritance tax arrangements should not override personal or commercial factors.

## Trusts

You may wish to 'skip a generation' and put funds in trust for grandchildren.

No one type of trust will suit all requirements. Life tenant, discretionary, and accumulation and maintenance trusts are all valuable tools in the right circumstances. The three main types can be summarised as follows:

1. If the need is to make lifetime gifts of shares in a family company for the benefit of specified individuals who are over the age of 25, while retaining control of the shares, then a gift to a life tenant trust with suitably chosen trustees may be the answer.

2. If the wish is to benefit children or young adults under the age of 25, then an accumulation and maintenance trust is probably the answer. The original settlement will be a potentially exempt transfer (free of tax if the settlor survives seven years), and no inheritance tax liabilities on eventual distribution of assets will arise. Although the beneficiaries must have a right to income by age 25, the trustees can retain control over the capital.

3. The most common use for a discretionary trust is likely to be for relatively small amounts of capital (within the nil rate tax band or for assets in excess of the nil rate tax band that qualify for 100 per cent

business or agricultural property relief). Such transfers should escape the periodic and distribution charges. It may be particularly useful as a mechanism in the will of the first spouse to die for giving the survivor access to income whilst keeping the assets out of his or her estate. It is particularly important to consider transfers into a discretionary trust of business or agricultural assets that currently qualify for the 100 per cent rate of relief. This would avoid the possibility of the rate of relief that may apply on a future death being less than 100 per cent. When the assets are settled on discretionary trusts, they will normally qualify for capital gains tax gifts holdover relief (see page 94).

## *Appendix I*

# Taxpayer's Charter

In August 1991 the Inland Revenue and Customs and Excise jointly published the Taxpayer's Charter, shown below.

**You are entitled to expect the Inland Revenue and the Customs and Excise**

**To be fair**
By settling your tax affairs impartially
By expecting you to pay only what is due under the law
By treating everyone with equal fairness

**To help you**
To get your tax affairs right
To understand your rights and obligations
By providing clear leaflets and forms
By giving you information and assistance at our enquiry offices
By being courteous at all times

**To provide an efficient service**
By settling your tax affairs promptly and accurately
By keeping your affairs strictly confidential
By using the information you give us only as allowed by the law
By keeping to a minimum your costs of complying with the law
By keeping our costs down

**To be accountable for what we do**
By setting standards for ourselves and publishing how well we live up to them

**If you are not satisfied**
We will tell you how to complain
You can ask for your tax affairs to be looked at again
You can appeal to an independent tribunal
Your MP can refer your complaint to an Ombudsman

**In return, we need you**
To be honest
To give us accurate information
To pay your tax on time

*Appendix II*

# Official Errors

In some cases tax which is due but has not yet been collected is waived if it arises because the Inland Revenue fails to make proper and timely use of information supplied by a taxpayer. This concession does not usually apply if the taxpayer is given notice of the tax arrears by the end of the next fiscal year following that in which it arose. The amount of the tax arrears waived will depend upon the gross income of the individual. For arrears which are first notified after 17 February 1993 the amounts waived are shown in Table 27.

Table 27 *Percentages of tax arrears waived because of official errors*

| Gross income £ | % of arrears waived |
|---|---|
| Not exceeding 15,500 | 100 |
| 15,501 – 18,000 | 75 |
| 18,001 – 22,000 | 50 |
| 22,001 – 26,000 | 25 |
| 26,001 – 40,000 | 10 |
| Exceeding 40,000 | 0 |

This practice applies to income and capital gains tax of individuals.

# Kidsons Impey Offices and Contacts

**Aberdeen**
11 Albyn Place
Aberdeen   AB1 1YE
Tel: (01224) 212222
Fax: (01224) 210190
Contact: Jim Braid

**Altrincham**
2 The Downs
Altrincham
Cheshire   WA14 2PX
Tel: (0161) 928 4391
Fax: (0161) 926 8169
Contact: Alan Ramsey

**Aylesbury**
Clock and Chimes Courtyard
2 Rickfords Hill
Aylesbury
Bucks   HP20 2RX
Tel: (01296) 432755
Fax: (01296) 433274
Contact: Howard Machin

**Beverley**
Carmichael Chambers
1 Wood Lane
North Bar Within
Beverley
North Humberside   HU17 8BS
Tel: (01482) 867951
Fax: (01482) 863577
Contact: Mike Holland

**Birmingham**
Bank House
8 Cherry Street
Birmingham   B2 5AD
Tel: (0121) 631 2631
Fax: (0121) 631 2632
Contact: Malcolm Garner

**Blackburn**
Parkgates
52A Preston New Road
Blackburn
Lancs   BB2 6AH
Tel: (01254) 674222
Fax: (01254) 674223
Contact: John Bury

**Boston**
100 Wide Bargate
Boston
Lincolnshire   PE21 6SE
Tel: (01205) 362405
Fax: (01205) 360529
Contact: David Hamshaw

**Bristol**
10 Apsley Road
Clifton
Bristol   BS8 2SP
Tel: (0117) 9730285
Fax: (0117) 9238456
Contact: Geoff Gollop

**Chelmsford**
Carlton House
31-34 Railway Street
Chelmsford
Essex  CM1 1NJ
Tel: (01245) 269595
Fax: (01245) 354285
Contact: Derek Jordan

**Chester**
Steam Mill
Chester  CH3 5AN
Tel: (01244) 327171
Fax: (01244) 317417
Contact: Graham Garner-Jones

**Coventry**
Park House
Station Square
Coventry  CV1 2NS
Tel: (01203) 256333
Fax: (01203) 222101
Contact: John Leech

**Derby**
6 Vernon Street
Derby  DE1 1FR
Tel: (01332) 360808
Fax: (01332) 384801
Contact: Matt Henderson

**Edinburgh**
23 Queen Street
Edinburgh  EH2 1JX
Tel: (0131) 225 6424
Fax: (0131) 220 1282
Contact: David Kipling

**Glasgow**
Breckenridge House
274 Sauchiehall Street
Glasgow  G2 3EH
Tel: (0141) 307 5000
Fax: (0141) 307 5005
Contact: Mike Blyth

**Grimsby**
27 Osborne Street
Grimsby
South Humberside  DN31 1NU
Tel: (01472) 351171
Fax: (01472) 240458
Contact: Keith Atkinson

**Hereford**
Elgar House
Holmer Road
Hereford  HR4 9SF
Tel: (01432) 352222
Fax: (01432) 269367
Contact: Tom Davies

**Horsham**
Peel House
Barttelot Road
Horsham  RH12 1BW
Tel: (01403) 251666
Fax: (01403) 251466
Contact: Sheena Sullivan

**Hove**
Enterprise House
83a Western Road
Hove
East Sussex  BN3 1LJ
Tel: (01273) 720311
Fax: (01273) 205453
Contact: Paul Hopwood

**Hull**
Dunedin House
45 Percy Street
Hull  HU2 8HL
Tel: (01482) 327406
Fax: (01482) 326957
Contact: Andrew Mould

**Ipswich**
Friars Courtyard
30 Princes Street
Ipswich
Suffolk  IP1 1RJ
Tel: (01473) 216154
Fax: (01473) 231586
Contact: Jonathan Penn

**Leeds**
Barclays House
41 Park Cross Street
Leeds  LS1 2QH
Tel: (01132) 422666
Fax: (01132) 422038
Contact: David Harrison

**Lerwick**
122 Commercial Street
Lerwick
Shetland Isles  ZE1 0HX
Tel: (01595) 693384
Fax: (01595) 695902
Contact: Bob Steele

**London**
Spectrum House
20-26 Cursitor Street
London  EC4A 1HY
Tel: (0171) 405 2088
Fax: (0171) 831 2206
Contact: Anne Gregory-Jones

**Manchester**
Devonshire House
36 George Street
Manchester  M1 4HA
Tel: (0161) 236 7733
Fax: (0161) 236 7020
Contact: Graham Kidson

**Norwich**
Fulcrum House
7 Norwich Business Park
Whiting Road
Norwich
Norfolk  NR4 6DJ
Tel: (01603) 628767
Fax: (01603) 662077
Contact: Paul Muttitt

**Nottingham**
Park House
Kirtley Drive
Castle Marina
Nottingham  NG7 1LQ
Tel: (0115) 9473002
Fax: (0115) 9473062
Contact: Terry Johnston

**Solihull**
618 Warwick Road
Solihull
West Midlands  B91 1AA
Tel: (0121) 711 3939
Fax: (0121) 711 4151
Contact: John Cooper

**Spalding**
Welland House
High Street
Spalding
Lincolnshire PE11 1UB
Tel: (01775) 766205
Fax: (01775) 710512
Contact: David Gratton

**Tunbridge Wells**
Ruskin House
14 St John's Road
Tunbridge Wells
Kent  TN4 9NP
Tel: (01892) 511944
Fax: (01892) 515852
Contact: Eddie Battarbee